# creation and reality

# michael welker

# creation and reality

Fortress Press      Minneapolis

CREATION AND REALITY

Translated by John F. Hoffmeyer

Scripture quotations are from the New Revised Standard Version Bible, copyright © 1989 by the Division of Christian Education of the National Council of Churches of Christ in the United States of America. Used with permission.

Cover design: Joseph Bonyata
Book design: Peregrine Graphics Services

0-8006-2628-1

The paper used in this publication meets the minimum requirements of American National Standard for Information Services—Permanence of Paper for Printed Library Materials, ANSI Z329.48-1984.

Manufactured in the U.S.A.                                                          1-2628
03   02    01    00    99        1    2    3    4    5    6    7    8    9    10

*To my Princeton friends and colleagues*

# contents

# acknowledgments

The chapters of this volume, all examining central themes of the doctrine of creation, were first formulated as lectures in the United States. Five entered the forum of public discussion as the Warfield Lectures at Princeton Theological Seminary. I am very grateful for the continued good exchange, both professional and personal, with colleagues there—including the Bible and Theology Project and the Consultation on Science and Theology.

The chapter on Genesis 1 and 2 was first conceived for the Annual Meeting of the Society of Biblical Literature and the American Academy of Religion in autumn 1990 in New Orleans (as part of a series on "Reinterpreting Classic Texts"). I have reworked the earlier lecture on the basis of lectures delivered as part of the same event by Phyllis Trible of Union Theological Seminary and Paul D. Hanson of Harvard Divinity School. I put forward an expanded version for discussion by colleagues of the Evangelical and Catholic Faculties of the University of Münster at their 1991 Epiphany Conference. I am grateful to them as well for fruitful provocation to further reflection.

A doctoral seminar held jointly with Jürgen Moltmann several years ago in Tübingen, and especially a paper delivered by Hartmut Gese at that seminar, made a valuable contribution to the chapter on "God's angels" in the present volume. They helped move me to understand statements of faith that resist being fit into our contemporary forms of experience but that, on the basis of their logic, enable a circumspect questioning of our constructions of "reality."

Finally, I am grateful for discussions within the framework of courses taught by my colleagues and friends Christof Gestrich and Bernd Janowski, in which chapters for this volume were subjected to critical examination.

I thank my wife Ulrike Welker for many conversations concerning the material and for her great help in preparing the manuscripts. Dr. John Hoffmeyer translated these essays with great linguistic and theological sensitivity. He bore with my numerous improvements, revisions, additions, and reworkings with friendliness and patience. I am very grateful to him for many years of collaboration and would like to say publicly in this place what I have repeatedly communicated to him: I often find his translations better than the original.

# introduction

*The Collapse of Bourgeois Theism
and the Crisis of Religious Existence*

The major churches in Europe, and partly in North America as well, are currently experiencing the collapse of classical bourgeois theism. More and more people are turning away from belief in a personal figure who exists over and above this world, who has brought forth both himself and all reality, and who controls and defines "everything" without distinction. They no longer affirm the omnipotence and ubiquity of God. This collapse, which naturally gives rise to powerful countermovements—for example, fundamentalist ones—is hitting churches and cultures hard. Many institutions and many people are experiencing a crisis of landslide proportions.

Laments over this development mostly overlook the fact that almost all significant theologies of the twentieth century have actually worked toward this collapse. This has been a deliberate goal in the thought of Dietrich Bonhoeffer and Jürgen Moltmann, in many theologies of liberation, and in almost all feminist theologies. At least initial steps in this direction have occurred in the work of Karl Barth, Wolfhart Pannenberg, Eberhard Jüngel, and David Tracy, in process theologies, and in other thinkers and developments.

It was above all christological and trinitarian insights and questions that were determinative of the efforts to put an end to classical theism. A realistic knowledge of the unity, vitality, personality, effectiveness, and glory of the triune God was and is being sought. But insights also from the theology of law and from pneumatology, as well as metaphysical, moral, and political reasons, forced theism into question. A whole array of critical encounters and movements are thus collaborating in the collapse of this religious form of power. Yet instead of contentment and rejoicing at the success, perplexity and discouragement seem to be proliferating. Indispensable religious and normative foundations seem to be crumbling or to have crumbled already. It is no idol that has been toppled. Instead it seems to many people that God's own self has fallen.

## Theology of Creation: Questions in Biblical Perspective

In this situation it is necessary not to give up the christological, pneumato-logical, and other debates with classical theism but to supplement them in the area of the theology of creation. The alliance between theism and belief in the Creator must also be examined. This book offers initial steps toward correct-ing both the classical theistic caricature of God the Creator and a corre-sponding religious understanding of "reality." Taking their orientation from the biblical traditions, these chapters look for perspectives and ways to achieve a pre- or post-theistic understanding of God's creative power and of the cre-ation intended by God.

This sort of attempt to develop a biblical-theological orientation is admit-tedly disputed in contemporary systematic theology. Raising such ideas has met with considerable agreement but also given rise to energetic criticism both from the North American Thomistic Catholic quarter and from the German Neoprotestant quarter. David Burrell, for example, has objected to rethinking the God-creation relationship, preferring instead to emphasize "the 'distinc-tion' of God from the world . . . which creation is meant to secure. . . ."[1] That is *the* task of the theology of creation, while specific knowledge of creator and creature remains completely vague: "So the quintessential task becomes one of formulating that 'distinction' so as to assure the required transcendence, *while allowing us to have some notion of what it is we are referring to* in addressing 'the Holy One,' 'our Father,' or 'Allah Akbar.'"[2] As important as this concern may be for basic theistic moves in a Thomistically defined philosophy of religion, it ought not to be advanced as a formulation of *the* fundamental task of the theology of creation.

One sees an analogous move in the thought of Eilert Herms.[3] Herms uses his so-called relation of existential grounding to argue against my analyses and to claim that the task of the theology of creation is to secure "the distinction" between God and creature. But his view of what he calls the "relation of cre-ation" as a twofold "relation of existential grounding"[4] is reductionistic in such a way that, like the conceptions that I examine in the following pages, it obscures a decisive point of the classical creation accounts: In concerning fundamental relations among creatures, both the interdependencies and the difference between creator and created can and must be recognized. To put things in a clear, straightforward and formal way: "The relation" between cre-ator and creatures cannot be illuminated in abstraction from the fundamen-tal "relations" between complex structural associations of creaturely existence. Inasmuch as Herms obscures this with his twofold "relation of creation," he performs precisely what I call false abstraction.

As much as I understand these defensive reactions, the objections have not persuaded me concerning the issues in question. They have not dissuaded me from my conviction that the dominant fundamental concepts and theoretical models of Christian theology again need to be subjected to a critique on a biblical-theological basis. This "Reforming" orientation is still relevant and promising today. The fruitful renewal of broad areas of Roman Catholic theology on an exegetical basis after the Second Vatican Council confirms me in my view, as do many good experiences in interdisciplinary conversation, both within and beyond the confines of theology.

At any rate, those within the sphere of Christian theology who think they can do without the biblical sources in handling questions about the theology of creation can learn from Friedrich Schleiermacher, for example, that the "dissolution of the relationships among that which is finite" for the sake of the "relationship of the finite to the infinite" leads to mysticism "in the bad sense."[5] Analogously, the "dissolution of the relationships among that which is finite" for the sake of the "relationship of the infinite to the finite" leads to a theism "in the bad sense," a theism that hardly provides perspectives on real tasks of the theology of creation.

As a by-product, the investigations presented here show that orienting theology on biblical traditions ought not to be abandoned in favor of an orientation on this or that "natural" theology of various times and cultures. To be sure, the biblical traditions themselves include diverse "natural" theologies. But in doing so they always expose themselves to the associated conflicts that arise in the search for truth between various rationalities and various understandings of reality.

## The New Biblical Theology

The investigations presented here count themselves among the new approaches of a "Biblical Theology" that have been developing in interdisciplinary and interconfessional collaboration since the 1980s, particularly in Germany and North America.[6] These approaches depart from all earlier attempts to take a single form—for example, personalism, existentialism, social criticism—or a single theme—for example, reconciliation, covenant, reign of God, God's glory—and to highlight it as *the* form or *the* content of the biblical traditions, or to read it into those traditions. Instead these approaches are consciously pluralistic. They take seriously the diverse biblical traditions with their different situations in life, with the continuities and discontinuities in their experiences and expectations of God, since those experiences and expectations are sometimes compatible with each other and sometimes not directly so.

The new approaches to a biblical theology are interested in these differences not only because they feel themselves intellectually obligated to excavate what are, from a historical-critical perspective, diverse "past presents." These new approaches have a burning theological interest in these differences because they are seeking to work out a tension-laden typology of inquiry and speech about God—a typology that gives rise to permanent self-criticism and to creative reconstruction. Precisely those tensions between relative commonalities and relative differences in the expectations and experiences of God in the different biblical traditions are essential to theological self-criticism. They are essential for theology's neverending task of distinguishing materially appropriate speech about God from religious projections and wishful fantasies.

Inasmuch as the new approaches to biblical theology, in their search for relative commonalities and continuities, do not seek to dissolve the differences in the biblical traditions, they gain bases for realistically reconstructing complex theological and key religious concepts and sets of concepts. They put themselves in a position where they are able to restore importance and orienting power to complex theological concepts that have had their cutting edge dulled by "natural" and so-called philosophical theologies in favor of reductionistic clarity.

The new approaches to biblical theology also proceed from the assumption that many of the biblical traditions' concepts and sets of concepts (for example, creation, world, sin, atonement, sacrifice, righteousness, reign of God, God's Spirit), which once possessed great orienting power, have now been so dulled by multiple accommodations to prevailing habits of thought and specific conceptions of rationality and moral systems that they function only as ciphers. This dulling of fundamental theological concepts is fatal not only to religious existence and the churches. It also robs cultures and societies of fundamental sources of orientation and important possibilities for self-criticism. "Religion" then becomes empty, boring, vapid, and banal, and so the augurs of the spirit of the age (even when they themselves operate with highly reductionistic forms of thought) lament theology's "lack of cultural competence."

This situation is not altered when theology attempts to abandon its central traditions, historicizing them away. Nor is it altered when theology attempts to refurbish the ciphers and the empty and hollow sounding "great words" by developing their rhetorical impact, heightening their entertainment value, or employing them to strengthen moral attitudes. Instead theology must direct all its powers toward uncovering the achievements of the central contents of faith in providing substantive orientation in diverse historical contexts. The chapters that follow attempt to do so through central examples drawn from the theology of creation. I would like to show that many of the biblical traditions' fundamental concepts dealing with the theology of creation provide stimuli and insights that are far from being exhausted—even in today's situation, where it is impossible to get a clear cultural overview and where ecological perplexity is the order of the day. In addition, these biblical concepts impel us to new and clearer knowledge of God and self in a time and world after the collapse of classical theism—which is to say, in our time and our world.

# chapter 1

# What Is Creation?
# Rereading Genesis 1 and 2

Do the great biblical creation accounts in fact agree with the guiding images and concepts of "creation" that we presuppose and use in Western religious and secular-cultural contexts?[1] Do Genesis 1 and 2 support the concepts of creation that our theological discourse as a rule also assumes and employs?

I have been greatly surprised to discover major divergence between, on the one hand, the concepts of creation implicit in Genesis 1 and 2, which are normative creation texts for the Jewish-Christian traditions, and on the other hand, the concepts of creation that are dominant in Western cultures. To be sure, Genesis 1 and 2 are not the only texts of the biblical traditions that speak about creation. But for Judaism they count—I quote Shemaryahu Talmon— as "the normative Hebrew creation tradition."[2] Genesis 1 and 2 are also regarded in Christian churches and in the areas of their cultural influence as the orienting foundation for knowledge and talk about creation. Even to the present day, exegetical and systematic efforts to mine the content of creation take recourse to these texts. In other respects these efforts may be as far removed from one another as the founding of the doctrine of creation in Barth's *Church Dogmatics*[3] and the important new contributions of feminist biblical interpretation of recent years[4] to the anthropology of the theology of creation.

Short and snappy, my thesis is this: A rereading of Genesis 1 and 2 shows the predominant conceptions of creation to be *false abstractions*. Over against the biblical texts, they are misleading, distorting definitions of creation. I shall attempt to ground this thesis in the first two parts of my reflections. The first part will bring before us the conventional, abstract conceptions of creation. In the second part, a rereading of Genesis 1 and 2 will shake up those guiding conceptions. The third part draws conclusions from that shake-up and seeks a more satisfactory answer to the question "What is creation?" In the fourth part I consider some anthropological consequences with regard to the relation between systematic theology, on the one hand, and exegetical and historical research, on the other. After reflecting on the consequences for both content and method that might be born of this investigation, I conclude by attempting to measure the limits of what we have undertaken.

# Conventional Guiding Conceptions of Creation

Secular common sense, as well as religious consciousness in the Jewish-Christian heritage, names creation the totality, the world, or nature, insofar as it is regarded as *produced* and *dependent*. The pattern of being produced and dependent remains a constant independently of whether the creation (*creatura*) is ascribed to a god, gods, or other more original, wholly superior, supra-mondane, and supernatural powers. Creation is the totality essentially conceived as nature. Or creation is nature that is produced by something superior and, on the basis of having been produced, is dependent.

Moreover, the act or the activity of producing the whole, the world, or nature is characterized as "creation" (*creatio*). The summarizing conceptions of, and ideas about, this act of production, and about what is thus produced, are very vague, mostly even obscure. These ideas are unfolded in myths, sagas, and several cosmogonical theories that are difficult to decode. In our culture these ideas have for a long time now been reduced to a very abstract and paltry conception of an ultimate process of causing and being caused, beyond which it is impossible either to go or to ask questions.

Little enough can be said about this ultimate process of causing and being caused. Merely two questions over and over again set in tired motion the obscure idea of an ultimate process of causing and being caused. These are questions that are familiar to the point of surfeit. First, are we to understand creation as creation out of *nothing*, or as creation out of absolute or relative chaos? Second, are we to conceive creation as a *one-time* act or as a *continuous* event?

The first question deals with the alternative between *creatio ex nihilo* and creation out of chaos. Is the activity of creation a qualitative leap—however we are to conceive it—from nothing to something? Is it a qualitative leap from a situation that offers no basis from which things can take shape, and about which nothing can be said, to a determinacy that is the beginning of any acquisition of understanding?[5] Or is the activity of creation a process of producing out of chaos? Is it a transformative process of producing higher aggregate conditions out of an absence of structure or relative lack of structure?

The second question deals with the alternative between creation at the beginning (*primordialis*) and *creatio continua*. Is the process of production and causation only the initial event for the course of the world? Or does it operate as an enabling condition in all that occurs?

In the past thought has futilely worn itself out working on these abstract alternatives, which resulted from a concept of creation that is too simple, too undifferentiated. The concept of creation that underlies these alternatives connects images of production and of the exercise of power. This concept enjoys universal currency even to the present day. It understands creation as a process of production beyond which it is impossible to go, and as absolute dependence.

"The doctrine of Creation has to do primarily with the ultimate dependence of all things on one transcendent reality." This formulation from Van Harvey is as succinct as it is representative.[6] Scholarly articles in major lexicons, such as those of Joseph Ratzinger and G. Gloege, admittedly warn against using the concept of causality and other basic abstract conceptions of production unreflectively. But then these articles use expressions like "posit," "originate," "free positing of the beginning," and so on, to define creation.[7] Over and over again it is assumed, wholly without hesitation, that this is the central insight of the Genesis creation texts. The recently published systematic theology of Kenneth Cauthen only repeats the conventional opinion when it sums up Genesis 1 with the words: "Its theological meaning is that the world depends absolutely on God for its origination and continuation."[8]

The doctrine of creation has fortified and passed on a simple pattern of power. This pattern of power presents creation as a process of being produced by a transcendent reality, a process of production behind which it is impossible to go. It presents creation as being in absolute dependence upon this transcendent reality. An ultimate process of being produced by a transcendent reality and absolute dependence—this pattern has been consciously regarded as that which alone is important and decisive in the doctrine of creation. Ferdinand Christian Baur, one of the most notable German theologians of the nineteenth century and a leading theoretician of historical-critical theology, enunciated this straightforwardly and without a trace of hesitation in his widely circulated *Manual of the History of Christian Dogma*. According to Baur, the doctrine of creation must "hold fast to the essential moment of the dependence of the world upon God." The "more determinate form of the same (namely, of this moment of dependence) no longer concerns Christian interest."[9]

Creation as an ultimate process of being produced by a transcendent reality and as absolute dependence upon that reality—this simple pattern of power has been accepted many times with a certain theological embarrassment and ignorance about where to turn. This shows itself, for example, in Leo Scheffczyk's introduction to the doctrine when he concludes that "the general consciousness both of an ultimate ground of things and of the dependence of human beings upon this ground . . . does not attain to what is specifically Christian about the truth of creation."[10] Yet here, too, that which is "specifically Christian" is grasped as a more precise determination, a heightening, a transcending of the basic pattern, which itself is not rendered fundamentally problematic.

Creation as an ultimate process of being produced by a transcendent reality and as absolute dependence upon this reality—this pattern of power also maintains itself in theologies that seek, with the help of other theological concepts, to develop and to render more precise the understanding of creation. Perhaps the best-known example of such an effort in this century is Karl Barth's attempt to bracket creation theology within covenant theology. To be sure, Barth's project differentiates and breaks in manifold ways the basic pattern of the powerful process of God's producing the creature, and of the absolute dependence of the creature on God. But Barth's project does not place that pattern in question as a basic pattern. Instead it remains an obscure *cantus firmus*, whether its derivation in the theology of creation is always clearly proved or not. "Creation" as an ultimate process of being produced by a transcendent reality and as absolute dependence upon this reality—these guiding conceptions are possibly untenable, a question we pose as we reread Genesis 1 and 2.

## Rereading Genesis 1 and 2

Neither Genesis 1 nor 2 describes God as a highest being who in pure self-sufficiency does nothing other than produce and cause creaturely being. Nor does either chapter describe creation as the totality, the world, or nature with the addition of an external ground, to which creation is related in mere dependence.[11]

In my estimation, the first surprising observation in the texts of Genesis 1 and 2 consists in the realization that God's creative action corresponds in only a few ways to the pattern of causation and production. By contrast, the texts are full of instances that emphasize and develop God's *reactive* experiencing and acting as God *reacts* to the presence of what is created. The texts describe in a differentiated way God's reacting through perception and evaluation. They describe God intervening in what is already created, intervening for the purpose of further specification.

Seven times the later creation account emphasizes God's *evaluative perception*: "And God saw that what had been created was good" (Gen. 1:4a, 10b, 12b, 18b, 21b, 25b, 31a). Three times Genesis 1 emphasizes God's activity of *naming* (Gen. 1:5a, 8a, 10a). Twice God intervenes in what is already created in order to *separate* it (Gen. 1:4b, 7b). The earlier creation account in Genesis 2 also inscribes God's creative activity with marks of reacting: God's self-binding to external events, actions, and presuppositions; God's interested observation; even God's learning. The creation account explicitly emphasizes that cultivated vegetation, an important goal of the creation event, is made dependent upon the cooperation of rain and of human activity. The creation account thus emphasizes that divine and human initiative coincide (Gen. 2:5). The creation account explicitly reserves for the human being—not yet differentiated into man and woman[12]—the naming of "all cattle, the birds of heaven and all animals of the field" (Gen. 2:19-20). The creation account explicitly emphasizes the validity of this fundamental, culture-creating human activity. "And as the human being named each being, so was it to be called" (Gen. 2:19b).[13]

Finally, God unquestionably acts in a reacting manner in response to the recognized need, the loneliness and helplessness, of the human being. The creating, sorting, and naming of the animals does not do away with that need. The differentiation of the human being into man and woman follows in an action that is described in detail, and in which it is as if God must outdo God's own self.

God saw, God evaluated, God named, God separated, God brought to the human being, God allowed to be named, God reacted to the needy situation of loneliness and helplessness of the human being who is not yet differentiated into man and woman. According to the classical creation texts, all these activities and reactivities are part of the complex event "creation." All these reactive activities, which relate to what is already "produced," are requisite in order to bring the process of the creation of heaven and earth to a close. God sees, names, separates, reacts in a differentiated way to the situation and behavior of the human being. What a world lies between this important characteristic of divine creating in the classical creation texts and the concept of pure production and causation!

The creating God is not only the acting God, but also the reacting God, the God who responds to what has been created. The creating God is open to being confronted by the independence, the originality, even the need for improvement of that which has been created. Only a distorting abstraction can block out the fundamental characteristic, emphasized throughout, of God's action as action that reacts, as action that lets itself be determined. *Reaction in perception, evaluation, naming and separating intervention; reaction in giving space for the human being's own activity; reaction in removing a recognized situation of need that cannot be spontaneously averted without further ado—all this is creation, according to Genesis 1 and 2!*

Yet not only the *reactivity of the creating God,* but also the *creature's own activity* is blocked out by the concept of production and causation. Or if it is not blocked, it is at least only understood by being distorted to the point of unrecognizability. Genesis 1 and 2 describe the entire creation as in many respects having its own activity, as being itself productive, as being itself causative. *The creature's own activity, which is itself a process of production, is not only a consequence and result of a creation that is already completed. Rather it is embedded in the process of creation and participates in that process* (cf. esp. Gen. 1:11ff.). The Priestly creation accounts describe *the whole creation,* not only and not firstly human being, as itself active, separating, ruling, and imparting rhythm, as itself producing and giving life.

To be sure, in both creation accounts particular significance accrues to human action, especially to the human action of cultivating nature. To be sure, the process of creation also includes cognitive and normative, culture-creating human behavior, and is directed toward that behavior. This characteristic is demonstrated by the fact that the earlier creation account so strongly emphasizes the naming of the animals—a naming that grounds culture. It is also demonstrated by the fact that the later creation account has the entire process of creation moving toward the day of rest, the cradle of all cognitive and normative culture.

But at this point I would only like to point out that the participatory activity of the creature does not find expression only with regard to human being. It certainly does not find expression only with the mandate of dominion, which since 1967 and Lynn White has gained notoriety and been the subject of much discussion.[14] The themes of the mandate of dominion and of creation and Sabbath are in themselves highly complex and require their own separate discussions,[15] but the aspect of the creature's own activity and productivity can be made clear without regard to those themes.

Anxiety about the creature's own power being too great is apparently foreign to the classical creation texts of the biblical traditions. Anxiety about the creature's own power being too great tends to entrench itself behind the model of causation and dependence. Instead of that anxiety, we encounter in the classical creation texts *a rich description of the creature engaged in the activity of separating, ruling, producing, developing, and reproducing itself.* Not only God separates, but also the creature—including the firmament of the heavens, the gathering water, and the stars—assumes functions of separation (Gen. 1:6, 9, 18). Not only God rules, but also the creature—for example the stars—rules by the establishment of rhythm, differentiation, and the gift of measure and order (Gen. 1:14ff.). Not only God brings forth, but also the creature brings forth creature: animals of all species and plants in an abundance of species (Gen. 1:12, but also 11, 20, 24!). And the creature develops and reproduces itself, as is recorded explicitly and in detail with regard to plants, animals, and human beings.

Repeatedly the creature's own differentiated activity is practically set parallel with God's creative action, without ceasing to be the creature's own activity. Thus the vault of heaven is to separate the waters and to create and maintain space for the further formation and development of the creature (Gen. 1:6). Yet in the very next verse we read, entirely in the sense of the dependence and causation model of creation: "God made the vault and separated . . ." (Gen. 1:7). The lights in the vault of heaven are "to rule over day and night and to separate the light from the darkness" (Gen. 1:14). Parallel to this we read, corresponding to the dependence and causation model: "God made . . . lights . . . ; God set the lights in the vault of heaven" (Gen. 1:16-18).

On the one hand, the creation accounts emphasize, in the sense of the production and dependence model, that God made all species of land animals (cf. Gen. 1:21 and 25). On the other hand, for precisely this process the texts lay claim to the productive powers *of the earth* (Gen. 1:24).[16]

Now in all these cases one can attempt to rescue the conventional model of causation and production with the help of the famous "yes-but" swing.[17] It is no secret that this swing can move in two directions. One can grant that *yes*, on all levels the texts emphasize the creature's own activity of producing, indeed even of separating and ruling. *But* not only does God's word initiate the creature's own activity; God's making, doing, and creating surround and transcend the creature's own activity. God's activity keeps the creature's own activity dependent and under control. Yet in relation to this conventional model of divine power, the same move can be swung in the other direction. First one emphasizes that *yes*, God's initiative is beyond question throughout. And—with different degrees of clarity—God's creative activity, which can be understood in the sense of production and causation, is beyond question throughout. *But* we are to conceive this activity together with the creature's own differentiated activity, an activity that is frequently asserted for precisely the same processes of creation!

My own proposal opts for *neither* of these two directions. My own proposal aims rather at totally freeing ourselves from this false alternative into which the model of production and dependence has pressed us. My proposal aims at recognizing that the classical creation accounts are much less anxiously concerned about simple, one-to-one hierarchical models than are the religious and theological conceptions still dominant among us. My proposal aims finally at seeing that, on the level of the model of production and dependence, we do *not* arrive at a clear differentiation of God's activity and the creature's activity in the process of creation.

If one does not approach the classical creation accounts of Genesis with the distorting glasses of the production and dependence model, one will have to conclude the following:

1. On the one hand, those accounts describe God's creative action so that it is comprehensible not only as actively producing and causing. They present it as equally reactive: in perception, evaluation, naming; in coming back and changing that which is already created; indeed, in learning by experience.

2. On the other hand, in a highly differentiated way they connect God's creative activity of production with the creature's own varied activity. The creature for its own part separates, rules, brings forth, and reproduces itself. The creature's own activity is not only the result and consequence of God's action. It goes along with God's action. At times it even seems to be interchangeable with God's action. The creature's own activity is constitutively bound up in the process of creation.

Where the conventional guiding conceptions focus upon *one-sided hierarchical arrangement and absolute dependence,* the classical creation accounts emphasize the *connectedness and cooperation* of creator and that which is creaturely. In no way do the creation accounts of Genesis offer only the picture of the sheer dependence of all creatures on an agent who somehow brings forth all of them. God's creative action does not confront that which is created with completely finished facts. The creature's own activity as a constitutive element in the process of creation is seen in harmony with God's action.

Yet is it still possible on this basis to determine in principle what "creation" is? Is it still possible to differentiate sufficiently God's activity and the particular activities of the creature? I think that we can answer both questions positively, even when we have given up the overly simplistic model of production and dependence.

I begin with the following abstract, minimal determination: *creation is the construction and maintenance of associations of different, interdependent creaturely realms.* God creates by bringing different creaturely realms into fruitful associations of interdependent relations that promote life.[18] The creature is drawn into and bound up into the process of creation by developing and relativizing itself and thereby fruitfully bringing itself into these associations of relations of interdependence, without which the creature would not exist. This is to be briefly developed in the third part of my argument.[19]

## *What Is Creation?*

Both creation accounts describe with different weight and subtlety the *construction of associations of interdependent relations between different creaturely realms.* A simple systemic sphere is not yet creation. We should not put forward as "knowledge of creation" the interest in unearthing a simple basic structure, a basic quality in all reality. The different creaturely realms have to do with the relations of human beings and vegetation, with the relations of human beings and animals, and also with the community of different groups and species of animals, etc.[20]

Yet the Jewish-Christian traditions grasp and describe creation in a still more elementary way as an association of *different*, interdependent creaturely realms. What is in question is the statement, strange at first to secular sensibilities, that God created the world as "earth and heaven." That is, God created not only the reality to which human beings have relatively immediate access, the reality which they can perceive, of which they can gain an overview, and which they can physically manipulate: the earth.

For the common sense that is still dominant today, it sounds strange and even absurd to make the statement that creation consists not only of the earth but also of heaven, that God also created heaven. "Imagine, there's no heaven, it's easy if you try, no hell below us, and above us only sky," wrote John Lennon. Certainly it is easy to imagine that there is heaven only as "sky." We connect talk about the remarkable creature "heaven" with outdated conceptions of reality. We think of Copernicus and Galileo, and the defeats that theology and the church have suffered in the struggle with the ideas of natural science. The Astrodome model of the world, in which heaven overarches the earth like a half-sphere, still counts today as one of the most striking proofs of the naïveté of ancient cultures and of the great advances that we have made in the meantime.

Yet here as well, influential yet false abstractions have led us astray. To be sure, it is false to generalize the Astrodome model as a cosmological model. This model is merely the generalization of the form in which *common sense perceives the world as its environment, when it observes the world in an immediate, unsophisticated manner*. Of course, for common sense with its immediate perception, the sun still moves around the earth today, and heaven can indeed appear as a half-sphere. It is important to see that this impression of the world, this impression that common sense makes for itself, is relativized not only in modernity, and not only by research in the natural sciences. Even in antiquity, the most diverse cultures, and without a doubt the biblical traditions, used the expression heaven to summarize *different* conceptual realms and different relational systems.[21] Thus in many biblical texts heaven and sky are almost identical, but in others the conception of earth includes the atmosphere, and heaven is only the realm of stellar constellations. Still other texts name the entire observable cosmos "the visible" and differentiate it from the "invisible heavens." The invisible heavens are disclosed in images, ideas, and even theories that today, in a primarily secular perspective, we regard as images, ideas, and theories about *power structures*, to the extent that we are able to decode them at all.[22]

I do not wish to speculate now about how perfectly or imperfectly the biblical traditions thought through these different relational systems in their connection with each other. I do not wish to speculate about how the unifying talk of heaven and the pluralizing talk of "the heavens" are related to each other in specific cases. I would like, though, to point out that Genesis 1 presents a sensorium for a more exacting conception of heaven. It does so by making the following distinction. On the one hand, Genesis 1 distinguishes the creation of light, which provides the more fundamental differentiation of light and darkness (Gen. 1:3ff.). On the other hand, Genesis 1 distinguishes the creation of the vault of heaven and the stars, which separate day and night, and thereby in a particular way separate light and darkness yet again (Gen. 1:14ff., esp. 1:18). From a purely systematic evaluation of this distinction one could conclude that here an "absolute" conception is being combined with a relative view, which is bound to a particular perceptual standpoint and to life on the earth. The absolute conception is expressed by the image of light and darkness prior to any further fashioning of the world (Gen. 1:3ff.). The relative conception is expressed by the Astrodome model with its alteration of day and night (Gen. 1:14ff.) At least systematically and in principle, here lies the basis for connecting monistic and pluralistic conceptions of heaven (and thus of the world).

At this point I would not like to pursue further the question of the linkage of unifying and pluralizing, relativistic conceptions of heaven. This is the question of the relation of religious and cosmological heavens, on the one hand, and the heavens of our perception, on the other hand. At this point I would not like to pursue further the relation of absolute and relative totality.[23] What is important to me is to give fundamental emphasis to the following point. From the word "Go," "creation" has in view the association of heaven and earth as interdependent realms, which are themselves internally differentiated.[24] In this way the realm of heaven is seen not only as the place from which *natural* forces—light, warmth, water, wind, and storm—determine life on this earth. Heaven is also seen as a place from which proceed strong forces that shape and determine *culture*.[25] In Genesis 1 we find this clearly expressed in the statement that the lights are "to be signs and to serve the determination of festivals, of days and of years" (Gen. 1:14). Other traditions and texts elaborate much more the images of the powers that proceed from heaven, whether these powers be natural, cultural or culture-determining. So far we have had great difficulty in deciphering some of those images and relating them to our own experience.

"Creation" is the construction of associations of interdependent relations between creaturely realms that are relatively accessible to us and those which are relatively inaccessible to us. The expression "heaven" synthesizes the natural *and* cultural realms over which we cannot exert direct influence. The realms that are more accessible to us, integrated by means of the expression "earth," are likewise grasped not only as natural but also as cultural associations of interdependent relations. In both creation accounts we find texts that point to the interdependence of that which we call nature and culture. For example, there is in both creation accounts the charge to human beings to cultivate the earth. There is the centering of creation upon the day of rest, which is blessed and in its own way fruitful. There is the giving of names to the animals, but also the "geographical" and "geological" elements in the description of the Garden of Eden (Gen. 2:10ff.). *A merely naturalistic understanding of creation does not attain the level of the classical creation texts. Creation is thus the construction and maintenance of associations of interdependent relations between those natural and cultural creaturely realms that are accessible to our formative influence, and those that are not accessible.*

From here let us cast a glance back to the old model of production, causation, and dependence. In doing so we see that the old model lacked the power to draw adequate distinctions and to make adequate contrasts. On the one hand, there are relations of dependence among creatures. On the other hand, there is the relation of creator to creature. The old model did not allow us to distinguish sufficiently between these two types of relation. Moreover, on the one hand there is the *creator's relation of transcendence to the creature.* On the other hand, there are instances of *relative transcendence* among creatures, grounded in the relation between heaven and earth. The old model did not allow us to contrast sufficiently these two types of transcendence.

That means, though, that the conventional conception of creation was insufficiently subtle, differentiated, and complex. For this reason its powers of theological disclosure and clarification came up wanting. First, within this conception dwells a compulsion to homogenize the creature over against the divine, a compulsion to turn the creature into a simplistic abstraction. On the one side is the divine that brings forth; on the other, the dependent creature. By comparison, the creation accounts are much more subtle. They require us to recognize relations of interdependence between a *plurality* of different creaturely realms. Second, the old conception misleads us into confusing or equating relations of dependence among creatures and the relation between creator and creature. The old conception is thus to a high degree susceptible to idolatry and ideology. One need think only of the widespread confusion of God and the "beyond," of God and heaven, or of the equally widespread undifferentiated talk of "transcendence." By contrast, the creation accounts reconstruct irreversible relations of dominion *in* the realm of the creaturely and at the same time counteract the divinization of the powers of heaven or of the monsters from the deep.

The stars and the "great sea monsters," the *taninim*, are not gods on high or anti-gods from the deep. They are—mere creatures. Gen. 1:21 explicitly emphasizes that God created the "great sea animals," the *taninim*,[26] while otherwise, as has often been observed, the account does not mention any particular species. Gen. 1:16ff. emphasizes that God made and secured in the heavens the stars that rule and that separate light from darkness. These emphases provide a religious critique in serving as reminders of the possibility of such divinizations and idolizations. By contrast, the creation account unmasks eerie phenomena (with regard to the sea monsters) and relations of dependence (with regard to the stars) as associations within the realm of the creaturely. Divinizations or idolizations of the luminary powers from on high, or of the powers of chaos from the deep, are sublated—in the full Hegelian sense. These divinizations and idolizations are "reconstructed" as constitutive parts of associations of interdependent relations among creatures.

The creation accounts of Genesis make us sensitive to relations of interdependence among creatures. They also make us sensitive to relations of power and transcendence among creatures. At the same time they lead us to direct more interesting and instructive questions to God and God's creative action than those which were fixated on the indeterminate power of production, causation, and dependence. These more interesting questions concern divine intentions and goals in the construction and maintenance of associations of interdependent relations among creatures.

What traits of justice, permanence, and validity, what forms of power, what dynamics do we recognize in the associations of interdependent relations among creatures? Which of them can be religiously and theologically qualified and which cannot? Which of them work against God's recognizable intentions?[27] It is not difficult to see that such questions do much more to activate and to challenge the world of religious symbols than do the questions that were possible and customary in the framework of the simple model of production and dependence.

On at least four points, it seems to me foreseeable that the proposed new understanding of the concept of creation will lead us forward in contemporary investigations.

1. It allows us to develop further and to render more precise the numerous recent efforts to recognize analogies between religious and ecological forms of thought and experience.[28]

2. It opens our eyes to see that knowledge of creation must focus essentially upon the interdependencies of natural and cultural processes.[29]

3. It makes us attentive to a fundamental difference between knowledge of creation and a scientific knowledge of nature, which aims at discovering an ultimate, simple, measurable, fundamental quality (a concept of nature that not only common sense and technology but also many theologies and philosophies still seem to hold as a normative and worthwhile goal ).[30]

4. It renders us sensitive to the exciting connection in the classical creation texts between absolute and relative totalizations, between
   monistic and pluralistic thought.[31]

Yet these are only initial examples of the places in which a change in fundamental religious and theological patterns of thought can also stimulate and
require the renovation and reconstruction of normative and cognitive structures in secular thought.

## Critique of Abstraction as a Theological Task

"You cannot think without abstractions; accordingly, it is of the utmost importance to be vigilant in critically revising your modes of abstraction."[32] Alfred
North Whitehead in his main philosophical works repeatedly pointed out that
our thought and our culture are guided by a bundle of conscious and uncon-
scious abstractions, which determine the possibilities and limits of our experience and action. He defined the chief task of philosophy as the discovery and
critique of these abstractions.[33] But he also saw that "sometimes it happens
that the service rendered by philosophy is entirely obscured by the astonish-
ing success of a scheme of abstractions in expressing the dominant interests of
an epoch."[34] Whitehead warned that "a civilization which cannot burst
through its current abstractions is doomed to sterility after a very limited
period of progress."[35]

To my mind it is time to uncover, and where appropriate, to criticize and
revise the abstractions that also determine our thought and behavior in the
areas of religious life, religious studies, theologies and scholarly occupation
with religious themes. I am also of the opinion that we cannot continue to
leave this task to philosophy alone, indeed not even to a freely operating systematic theology. The task of laying bare and, where appropriate, of criticizing and revising our guiding abstractions seems to me rather to be an interdisciplinary task.

At issue is an interdisciplinary task, because the abstractions with which
we are confronted are located and operate in several contexts: namely, in texts,
in dogmatics, in the communication of religious communities, in common
sense's external perspective on religion, etc. The guiding abstractions are powerful precisely because they function in different contexts that mutually support and strengthen each other—or that mutually hinder and debilitate each
other. They are powerful in their vitality and powerful even in their ossifica-
tion. Their uncovering and their revision are, if successful, of extreme consequence. Therefore it is neither possible nor permissible to allow the important

process of the critique of abstractions to remain left up to a single discipline and perspective.

Researchers who have learned to work with patterns of thought and with systematic structures must cooperate with other scholars who are schooled in elucidating texts or in reconstructing historical and contemporary contexts. They must cooperate with other scholars who understand the operative powers of symbols in practical and political realms. In order to attack the great and momentous task of laying bare our guiding religious abstractions and criticizing them under present conditions, we need interdisciplinary cooperation between persons who are schooled in exegesis, systematic theology, and social sciences.

To be sure, one can shrink back in fear from this task. Guiding conceptions have been handed down to us and have been finely tuned by long use. Calling those conceptions into question can easily knock loose an avalanche of resultant problems. If we call attention to how much our guiding abstractions, our classical and normative texts, and the conscious attitudes of our common sense have diverged from each other, we can quickly fall into the whirlpool of relativism. In our time and in our cultures it is in no way a foregone conclusion that we orient our guiding conceptions, even our guiding religious conceptions, on biblical texts. For example, suppose we point out the abyss that separates our conceptions of creation and our most important creation texts. The question immediately poses itself in our culture whether, for example, we ought not rather take recourse to philosophical classics or cosmological theories or complex contemporary problems, in order to reformulate guiding abstractions or to acquire new abstractions. Uncertainties arise. To which theories ought we to take recourse? From which epochs? From which disciplines? On what grounds? Questions present themselves. Who selects and formulates the problems? How are we to guarantee the adequacy of their reality and complexity?

I very much understand the fear that greets this explosion of resultant problems. Yet I would like to submit an emphatic plea not to fear that explosion more than life with ossified, false abstractions, not to fear that explosion more than the sterility brought by a disengaged intellectual, religious, dogmatic, and confessional routine. The signs of decay in the major classical churches of the Western industrial nations and the erosion of classical bourgeois theism should be perceived as indications of such a deadly routine.

By contrast, this work seeks to use one example to draw attention to the great possibilities for change in our guiding theological conceptions that lie in the biblical texts. It is astounding what possibilities for the critique and transformation of guiding abstractions show themselves even in a very limited look at a very short passage (primarily Genesis 1).[36]

For my view was indeed very limited. My cultural heritage and surroundings of course impose limits upon my capacity for theological perception and imagination. Apart from those limits, my view was limited by an exclusively "literary approach," which exegetical research will surely correct and expand. It was further limited, and strongly so, because to a large extent I bracketed out the complex anthropology of the doctrine of creation, as well as the thematic cluster centered upon the Sabbath, with all the consequences of that thematic cluster.[37]

If in spite of the limitation of my view and in spite of the thematic reduction, we can already identify such clear and powerful alternatives to well-honed, false abstractions with regard to creation, the project of a biblically oriented interdisciplinary revision of our dominant abstractions seems to me to be enticing and encouraging.

Considered through the murky glass of hardened abstractions, the biblical traditions certainly can seem like a heap of rubble, or like museum pieces that have come to us from some distant recess of the world. Yet these same traditions also harbor possibilities for the critique and transformation of theological, religious and secularized abstractions that continue to guide us even today. In the light of *transformed* abstractions the apparent rubble heaps and museum pieces present themselves very differently. They present themselves as developed forms and witnesses of a life that is permeated by knowledge. They radiate and provide orientation even into our future, full of innovative power and full of wisdom.

# chapter 2

# Creation and the Problem of Natural Revelation

Is it true that contemporary common sense sometimes understands "creation" as nature, and sometimes as reality or "the whole"? If so, then in its understanding of creation this common sense lies in a dogmatic slumber from which it ought to be awakened.

The connection between creation and reality is differentiated and in need of clarification. On the one hand, we ought to guard against simply equating creation with vague conceptions of totality (the whole of reality, etc.). Creation is not simply "the whole." On the other hand, we ought to avert currently common identifications of creation with reductionistic understandings of reality. Creation is not merely nature or history or absolutely dependent existence. A theological approach that takes both these warnings seriously must consider the burden this places upon the relation between faith and experience. Such an approach claims, after all, that creation as encountered in experience does not manifest itself to us as totality or as nature or as history. Special cognitional efforts are required in order to distinguish creation from reality and to relate the two to each other. Why is this not an unnecessary complication but instead a fruitful problematization of a false creation security?

With the help of the perspicacious evaluation and critique of the concept of natural revelation developed by John Calvin, this chapter seeks to awaken common sense and a naive religious attitude from the dogmatic slumber in which creation, the whole, reality, nature, and other major concepts continually flow into each other. In the process it will also become clear why naive religious life and common sense find this slumber pleasant—and why they resist being awakened. The concept of natural revelation holds out the prospect of a bridge between belief in creation and the reality of experience. Who could want to attack this bridge? Before I present Calvin's insights, I would like to characterize the hopes that are placed in natural revelation. Finally, I would like to show the way in which creation and revelation are bound together and the way in which God's revelation in creation calls natural religious sentiment into question.

## The Defect of Revelation: Why Does Common Sense Prefer Natural Revelation?

We surely do not go astray in assuming that, from the perspective of the common sense that today can be presupposed in our cultures, the Christian language of revelation as the ground and basis of Christian experience and of the Christian knowledge of God calls forth at the very least discomfort. Common sense assumes that faith, by relating itself to revelation, admits that experience and knowledge of God do not go without saying and that they cannot be acquired without further ado. Since faith relates itself to revelation, faith maintains that experience and knowledge of God are not as easy to attain, to repeat and to render plausible as other experiences and instances of knowledge. In any case they cannot be attained, repeated, and rendered plausible with as much security as can other experiences and instances of knowledge. For example, experiences and instances of knowledge in our daily routine, having to do with objects of perception and persons in our immediate surroundings, are more accessible. That of course does not mean that in our daily life we only have to do with experiences that are obvious or easy to have and easy to communicate.

Indeed many experiences and instances of knowledge are difficult to clarify, difficult to reproduce, and difficult to render plausible. Mathematical operations, complicated experiments, encounters with foreign languages and cultures, complex personalities and texts give us examples of that. Yet in none of those cases do we talk about the necessity of a "revelation." In all those cases we can adduce specific methods and manners of proceeding that are necessary in order to attain or render optimal a specific instance of knowledge or a specific experience. In most of these cases we are acquainted with established, describable ways that allow us to reproduce the experiences or the instances of knowledge, or at least to attain a result analogous to them.

By contrast, the experience of God and the knowledge of God that are acquired by appeal to revelation seem to be of another sort. If that is so, the question arises whether it is legitimate to speak of experience and knowledge of God at all. Moreover, common sense harbors the suspicion that the concept of revelation is employed in order to veil the fact that there is no such thing as knowledge and experience of God that can be dependably communicated and comprehended, or that are even true. Inasmuch as human beings appeal to revelation, they seem to admit that both experience and knowledge of God are extremely unlikely. What prevents the conclusion from being drawn that an experience of God is imparted only to individual human beings who are somehow fortunate or peculiar or to human beings who are distant in either space or time, or in both space and time?

In this situation *natural* revelation appears as a compromise offer or even as an emergency rescue. After all, natural revelation says that revelation does not occur in a fully arbitrary and idiosyncratic manner. Rather it says that revelation is firmly tied to what is earthly and creaturely and that revelation can be incorporated into a manner of perception that is related to the earthly and creaturely. Rom. 1:19 and 20 can be regarded as Exhibit A for talk of natural revelation. There we read: "For what can be known about God is plain to them [human beings], because God has shown it to them. Ever since the creation of the world God's eternal power and divine nature, invisible though they are, have been understood and seen through the things God has made." In the works of creation are perceived God's invisible reality, God's eternal power and divinity. This trust in the religiously illuminating power of the works of creation seems to be shaken by our calling into question the unproblematic connection between creation and reality. Does not such questioning throw us back on an experience of God that is totally subject to "pious" caprice and speculation?

Chapters 3 to 5 of the first book of Calvin's *Instiitutes*[1] help us explain why revelation—but not "natural revelation"—takes up a position against the obscure, vague, presumptive, and dangerous elements of religions and theologies, including Christian religion and theology. Along with this, Calvin offers the most impressive critique known to me of all natural revelation and natural theology. He instructs us to be cautious in identifying creation and reality and provides clarity with reference to the supposedly Pauline talk of a so-called natural revelation.

## Calvin's Appreciation and Critique of Natural Revelation

Chapter 3 of the first part of the *Institutes* begins with the statement: "That there exists in the human mind, and indeed by natural instinct, some sense of Deity, we hold to be beyond dispute."[2] Presumably a contemporary reader will call this statement into question. With certain restrictions, the natural sense of deity may have been a viable presupposition over 400 years ago in the Reformation. But that it stands "beyond dispute" seems not to have been valid even then. After all, there have always been diverse hues of agnostics, skeptics, and critics of religion. Naturally Calvin knows that, for he cites agnostics, skeptics and critics of the faith in the *Institutes*. In any case it cannot be valid for us and for culture today that the presupposition of a natural sense of deity stands beyond dispute.

Yet if Calvin does in fact assume that there is—beyond dispute—"in the human mind, and indeed by natural instinct, some sense of Deity," then it is difficult to see how he is supposed to be able at all to arrive at a conception of revelation and to advocate a corresponding theology. Would not such a natural sense of deity make revelation completely unnecessary? If it is correct that the human mind possesses some sense of deity, would not an investigation of the human mind and its "naturally" given contents—instead of revelation—be the best path to the experience and knowledge of God?

So-called natural theology had indeed always said this: The human mind possesses by natural instinct some sense of deity. If Calvin could justify his statement, he would furnish a strong basis for a natural theology. Who needs revelation if the human mind possesses such an awareness through an instinct that is "natural," not something that must be arranged? Suppose, though, that Calvin was *unsuccessful* in proving this sense of deity. Suppose that we have to take as given the decline of natural theology. Then the question arises why the emphasis upon revelation is more than the ultimately futile attempt to save religion and theology from collapse. Thus in various ways the impression can be created that Calvin has generated only confusion for us today with his statement that it is beyond dispute that the human mind possesses by natural instinct some sense of deity.

If his statement were tenable, what would argue against the thesis that we should give up busying ourselves with supposedly particular contents of the faith and should instead stick to our immediately given experience? If his statement were not tenable, because we did not find anything in immediately given experience that referred us to God, to creator and creation, etc., then the retreat to revelation would appear to be a move of desperation that disavows the faith.

Yet all these disturbing objections disappear when one begins to understand that according to Calvin's insight, the sense of deity by means of a natural instinct in the human mind is *extremely vague*. When one begins to understand that, the arguments of the *Institutes* turn from being apparently weak and self-contradictory ones to being a strong defense of a theology of revelation. The sense of deity[3] is by no means clear. If we term this sense, as Calvin does, "knowledge of God," we must immediately join him in adding that this knowledge of God is "fleeting and vain."[4] It is not a matter of a specific knowledge of a specific God. It is *simply* a matter of a "sense of Deity." Yet by no means should we deduce from that a banal trivialization of this knowledge. Calvin is convinced that by no means can we or may we simply denigrate this sense of deity—however vague, however "fleeting and vain" it may be. Rather it is extremely important to recognize that this vague, futile, and fleeting knowledge, this instinctive sense is *extraordinarily powerful*, in spite of its constitution, which tends to provoke trivialization, denigration, and reduction to indifference.

It may astound us that this knowledge, this experience is so powerful, although one cannot really build reliably upon it. At issue is an awareness that is powerful in its seductive and tormenting presence: at times promising and encouraging, then again painful and distressing, sometimes lively, sometimes dull. The unspecific knowledge of divinity—however this knowledge affects us—is there and cannot be avoided. *It is a vague knowledge of a vague power that surrounds us in such a way that we can neither get a firm handle on it nor avoid it.* Psalm 139 addresses this power when it says: "You hem me in, behind and before, and lay your hand upon me" (Ps. 139:5). In the manner of a lament we read in Job 19:6 and 8: "Know then that God has put me in the wrong, and closed God's net around me. . . . God has walled up my way so that I cannot pass."

Calvin gives extremely graphic descriptions of this vague knowledge and of this natural religious sense when he addresses the situation of those who attempt to flee this sense.

> The most audacious despiser of God is most easily disturbed, trembling at the sound of a falling leaf.[5] How so, unless in vindication of the divine majesty, which smites their consciences the more strongly the more they endeavour to flee from it? They all, indeed, look out for hiding-places, where they may conceal themselves from the presence of the Lord, and again efface it from their mind; but after all their efforts they remain caught within the net.[6]

Calvin strikingly depicts how human beings are driven by anxiety of conscience, expressed only as a natural sense of God:

> Though the conviction may occasionally seem to vanish for a moment, it immediately returns, and rushes in with a new impetuosity, so that any interval of relief from the gnawings of conscience is not unlike the slumber of the intoxicated or the insane, who have no quiet rest in sleep, but are continually haunted with dire horrific dreams. Even the godless themselves, therefore, are an example of the fact that some idea of God (*aliqua Dei notio*) always exists in every human mind.[7]

Even if we today do not agree with Calvin in his description of the "godless," even if we regard his description as belonging to another time and as an expression of the religious propaganda of that time, Calvin's decisive point remains valid and important. The sensitivity and the restless activity of our consciousness indicate that we are all in a way ensnared in a reality that we cannot adequately control. We are ensnared in a reality with which we must struggle, or with which we think we must struggle, because it continually challenges us, surrounding us while refusing to be domesticated. Even the fear of death and the compulsion always to be on the run, such characteristic marks of modern consciousness,[8] bring to expression this struggle with that vague power that surrounds us in such a way that we can neither get a firm handle on it nor avoid it. *Unrest in the face of this power*—admittedly interrupted from time to time by a rest that is undependable, deceptive, and vanishing—*characterizes the natural sense of deity.*

Divinity as it comes through natural awareness does not meet us as something clear and determinate. We encounter it as a whole with some kind of order: not as a summit, a center, or a power with some kind of clear contours. It certainly does not encounter us as a clear person, for instance as a clear "Thou" writ large. It does not encounter us in the forms and patterns of our traditional theologies and varieties of piety. Instead it destroys those forms and patterns. Divinity as it comes through natural awareness is a vague power around us. In its ubiquitous vagueness and vague omnipresence it is a tormenting power. Psalm 139:7ff. registers the experience of this power—admittedly in the certainty that this vagueness and obscurity are not impenetrable for Godself:

> Where can I go from your spirit?
>     Or where can I flee from your presence?
> If I ascend to heaven, you are there;
>     if I make my bed in Sheol, you are there.
> If I take the wings of the morning
>     and settle at the farthest limits of the sea,
> even there your hand shall lead me,
>     and your right hand shall hold me fast.
> If I say, "Surely the darkness shall cover me,
>     and the light around me become night,"
> even the darkness is not dark to you. . . .

Calvin does not stop with his emphasis upon the vagueness and indeterminacy of the natural sense of deity. He unquestionably also describes factors that give certain *degrees of clarity* to this power, this sense of being hemmed in, this feeling of being inevitably surrounded. In particular Chapter 5 of Book I of the *Institutes* concerns itself with some of these relative clarifications of that which is felt to be an overwhelmingly powerful environment: the "beautiful order of the world," as Calvin says, the structures of nature, the order of our bodies, the accessibility of reality through our knowing, and so on. All these factors *point* to God's power and divinity. They point to a power that in a determinate manner transcends their own structures, forms, and complexities. In this manner, by pointing beyond itself, by pointing to a power that outdoes its own immunity to all attempts to exhaust it or domesticate it, creation gives witness to the creator! In Calvin's view it is precisely this that Paul has in mind when he writes in Rom. 1:20: "Since the creation of the world God's *invisible reality*, God's eternal power and deity, have been perceived in the works of creation."

Like other instances or parts of creation, natural religious sense gives witness to God's invisible nature and perceives that nature—admittedly in only a vague manner. Although this sense of deity can attain or make use of more or less developed forms, insights, and experiences, none of these insights is able to give rest, definitive guidance, or even contentment to our restless consciousness. Only problematic *degrees* of clarity, only degrees of fulfillment are attained. Even in the natural perception of God by means of the creation, human beings are referred back to God's revelation.[9] Even with regard to the testimony of creation, human beings are referred back to God's "invisible reality, God's eternal power and divine nature." On the basis of natural knowledge, human beings can never attain more than relative, problematic degrees of clarity with regard to that invisible reality.

One must mercilessly insist: On that basis human beings can never definitively distinguish between their fantasies and conceits and the true experience of God! Naturally, says Calvin, some human beings customarily dress up their superstition in pious terms: If it is an issue of religion and piety, then the presence of divinity can no longer be tormenting, and then human experience can no longer be fully inadequate! In the face of such pious illusions, Calvin's insight is of shattering sobriety:

> They deem it enough that they have *some kind* of zeal for religion, how preposterous soever it may be, not observing that true religion must be conformable to the will of God as its unerring standard. . . . [God] is no spectre or phantom, to be metamorphosed at each individual's caprice. . . . Those, therefore, who set up a fictitious worship, merely worship and adore their own delirious fancies; indeed, they would never dare so to trifle with God, had they not previously fashioned him after their own childish conceits. Hence that vague and wandering opinion of Deity is declared by an apostle to be ignorance of God.[10]

The sense of deity by means of natural instinct, proper to the human mind, remains vague or, as Calvin says, "unstable and fleeting." Since human beings must live with this condition, and yet cannot become happy with it, they feel compelled to make for themselves all sorts of idols. Or they attempt, albeit in vain, to suppress this instinct which brings forth the sense of deity:

> Even idolatry is ample evidence of this conception [that is, that a sense of Deity is pre-given]. For we know how reluctant human beings are to lower themselves, in order to set other creatures above themselves. Therefore, when they choose to worship wood and stone rather than be thought to have no God, it is evident

how very strong this impression of a Deity must be; since it is more difficult to obliterate from the human mind, than to break down the feelings of nature.[11]

It goes without saying that in our day this line of argumentation needs to be refined. One would have to accommodate it to our contemporary forms of idolization: our striving after money, success, and public recognition and resonance; perhaps our participation in fads and trends or our reverence for the so-called realistic constraints of a given situation. One would have to relate Calvin's line of argumentation to the systems of morality and the public opinions that we ourselves produce and at the same time idolize.[12] The gods and idols before whom we bow today and before whom we humble ourselves are no longer made of wood or stone. They are perhaps made of metal and paper and airwaves. They have set up camp in the mass media, in institutionalized rules of success, in moral and political routines. Or they are the gods of individual, regional, and national egoism: gods who are well-known and at the same time changing and difficult to grasp. As our environments give rise to feelings of dependence, their vague complexity oppresses us. There are many ways in which we seek to reduce this complexity, the complexity that constitutes our religious sense. There are many ways in which we construct, find, or select supposedly dependable powers that can direct our lives. Consciously or unconsciously, in piety or idolatry we strive for a clear and direct sense of God. Augustine characterized this striving and the unrest that accompanies it with the classic words: "My soul is restless until it finds its rest in Thee, O God." How can an end be made to the lack of orientation or the relativism of the self-made religious insights that proceed because of God's invisible nature?

## Creation and Revelation

It is important, especially for Christians and for theology, to face squarely the fact that in our cultures and in the life of individuals today there are not only numerous efforts but also numerous recognized solutions to the problems, described above, that arise in dealing with "natural revelation." There are religious and secular, public and private idolatries that offer us gods or various forms of replacements. These replacements are supposed to serve as ways for us to come to terms with our vague sense of being inevitably hemmed in and irremediably dependent. There are countless idolatries that help us to live with the sense of being surrounded by a complexity that leaves its determinative imprint upon us and that at the same time we cannot control. Besides the idols that are more or less easily grasped, cynical attitudes, rituals of indifference and of self-narcotization, and of course cultivated and uncultivated lethargy are at our disposal.

It would be naive to assume that this multiplicity of ways to suppress our religious sense could extinguish it. It would be no less naive to think that the constructive attempts to solve the problem posed by our religious sense with regard to "natural revelation" would gradually and automatically produce clear experience of God and clear knowledge of God. "I do not say with Cicero," writes Calvin, "that errors wear out by age, and that religion increases and grows better day by day. For the world . . . labours as much as it can to shake off all knowledge of God, and corrupts worship in innumerable ways."[13] In its vagueness, undependability, and inconstancy, "natural revelation" reveals the powerlessness of human beings: their inability to attain on their own a clear and determinate knowledge of God.

God's revelation leads human beings beyond this intention. Without that revelation we would have to persist in this web of relatively clear and relatively obscure religious and anti-religious endeavors. There are of course certain states of affairs and experiences, elements and structures of the world that seem to awaken, encourage, strengthen, and clarify our religious sense. But all these states of affairs, experiences, and structures ultimately fall back into vagueness and ambivalence. They remain in the grip of illusion; they remain open to misuse: "In vain for us, therefore, does Creation exhibit so many bright lamps lighted up to show forth the glory of its Author. Though they beam upon us from every quarter, they are altogether insufficient of themselves to lead us into the right path."[14]

Some defenders of a natural theology readily cite Psalm 19:2: "The heavens are telling the glory of God; and the firmament proclaims God's handiwork." They should not forget to add texts such as 1 Kings 8:27: "Even heaven and the highest heaven cannot contain you." Although there are so many "bright lamps" in the universe, they cannot lead us in a sure way to knowledge of God. Although we have a religious sense, a natural sense of deity, "we are deficient in natural powers which might enable us to rise to a pure and clear knowledge of God."[15] When we ask what mediates for us a clear knowledge of God, or what brings us on the straight way to knowledge of God, it is precisely not "natural revelation" to which we can refer. We must rather ask what happens with us in *God's* revelation—which also leads us beyond the status of merely "natural knowledge of God."

A number of theologies have emphasized that God's revelation is experienced in an *encounter*. This is variously presented as a personal encounter, a confrontation with God's otherness, a challenge, a process of being called and being taken captive, indeed a process of being addressed by that which is transcendent. This confrontation and encounter model is certainly not totally false and misleading. It is indeed strong in its negative power. It is strong in rejecting all theologies that begin with something arranged by human beings on their own, or even with only a self-examination of religiousness or something of the sort, in order thus to reach the experience of God and the knowledge of God. The model that regards God's revelation as encounter negates such attempts. It is God's appearing on and entering into the scene that sets human beings loose from themselves. Without that, human beings do not really come free of themselves and of their inability, rooted in their aggressively asserted finitude,[16] to know God. They cannot free themselves from the delusive structures that are strengthened by human beings' own activity.

Even the religious who are occupied with zealous attempts at self-detachment do not become free from *themselves*. Without the *discontinuation* of experience effected by God's appearing on and entering into the scene, human beings remain prisoners in themselves and in their reality. The encounter model has this intention of averting false paths, but it still does not offer any clear concept of God and God's revelation. In spite of the emphasis on the encounter and on the confrontation with God's otherness in revelation, the religious human being can still be thrown back into the vagueness of natural theology. Because the encounter model concentrates on only one aspect of revelation, albeit an important one, it is not strong enough to overcome the problems of natural revelation. It is not strong enough to explain how and why revelation mediates a clear knowledge of God. It is strong in its rejection of all conceptions that say that faith and trust have a healthy foundation in the fact that the human mind possesses "by natural instinct some sense of Deity." Yet it does not yet offer any clear alternative. How do we get to that point?

In general terms, revelation is disclosure, the emergence of something hidden, the proclamation of something unknown.[17] This indeed contains a moment of encounter and confrontation, of surprise and of the unpredictable. But encounter and confrontation do not necessarily contain disclosure, the emergence of something hidden, the proclamation of something unknown. The more substantial theologies of revelation thus emphasize not simply God's otherness and the fact that God is not at our disposal, according to our own arrangements. They call attention not to an abstract event of confrontation; they call attention to the *determinacy* of God's revelation: they emphasize the determinacy of the revelation in Jesus Christ, in the gospel, or in the coming of God's reign. In revelation we are confronted with a determinate name, a determinate power and reality, a determinate new reality. This determinate name, this determinate person, this determinate reality and history are the center of a realm of experience into which we are drawn. Revelation is thus not only a confrontation that, after it has happened, leaves us where we already were. Nor is revelation simply a piece of information or a bundle of particulars that is new to the human recipient of revelation and that instructs or in some other way partially enriches him or her.

Revelation, which includes determinate orientation, determinate knowledge, and determinate information, binds the human recipient of revelation and draws her or him *into a realm of experience that, without the intervention of revelation, was not there, or for the affected human being at least was not recognizable, was not really transparent, and did not really make an impact. Revelation draws us into a new and different realm of experience, into a new and different history, into a new and different personal and public identity, into a new reality.*

It is difficult adequately to grasp and to describe this complex reality and this complex experience. Centered on God's name, centered on Christ's person, we have a different knowledge and experience of ourselves and of the realities in which we live. We are transformed by revelation. Revelation grounds and opens up a new force field of experience, action and interaction, of which we become a part. But what prevents us on this level of knowledge from being thrown back again into the vagueness of natural theology?

Certainly for many human beings even today the vague talk that in faith a transformation, a creative transformation, a continual renewal occurs, sounds somehow promising and inviting. But can we explain to our fellow human beings that what is being talked about is not simply once again the birthplace of idols and illusions? As we self-critically come to grips with the handling of revelation, as we self-critically come to grips with the expectations that are to be directed at revelation, at this particular point great significance falls to the critical knowledge of *creation.*

Let us first note that we cannot directly transform the vagueness of the natural religious attitude into a substantial knowledge of God. But on the basis of revelation we can certainly recognize the vagueness of the natural religious attitude. We can get as far as suffering under our inability to arrive by our own power at clear knowledge of God. At the same time, God's revelation through creation drives us into determinate questions, into determinate knowledge of problems, into knowledge of associations of relations of power, dependence, and interdependence. This knowledge of associations of relations of power, dependence, and interdependence is what Paul means when he speaks of the apparently paradoxical *knowledge of God's invisible reality,* eternal power and divinity through the works of creation. Precisely that is what he means when he says that God reveals to human beings what can be known of God—and here we must supplement: *remoto Christo,* without Christ. Knowledge of creation is specific, differentiated knowledge of experiences of limitation, powerlessness, and finitude in realms of the creaturely. These realms and the corresponding experiences certainly include order and ordered well-being. But they do not provide direct access to God's *visible* reality or to a *finite* power that could mirror God's eternal power. The knowledge of creation can mediate such a revelation only in connection with the working of Christ and of the Holy Spirit.

Nevertheless, in the knowledge of creation vague, natural religious life is broken open, differentiated, and driven to manifold determinacy and manifold self-awareness. With that our ways of experiencing are altered. An altered force field conditions altered experiences and ways of experiencing. On the basis of revelation, determinate knowledge of being both powerless and sheltered and supported, determinate experiences of fundamental helplessness and fundamental trust replace the opaque, tormenting, global experience of dependence in the knowledge of creation. Knowledge of creation is without a doubt always knowledge of limitation, finitude, and powerlessness in the midst of experiences of superior power and might. To be sure, knowledge of creation is at the same time knowledge, rational perception, not collapse into a diffuse religious or nonreligious awareness,[18] into cognitive resignation, into routinized cynicism and indifference. With this cautious, broken relation to a natural knowledge of God transformable and transformed through revelation—a relation that one can learn from Calvin—I wish to attempt to unfold and to verify aspects of the knowledge of creation in the four remaining chapters of this volume. What effect do the powers "heaven and earth," angels, the so-called "mandate of dominion," and sin have over vague natural religious awareness?

# chapter 3

# Creation as the Heavens and the Earth

"If I have a system," wrote the early Karl Barth in the Preface to the second edition of his commentary on Romans, "it is limited to a recognition of what Søren Kierkegaard called the 'infinite qualitative distinction' between time and eternity, and to my regarding this as possessing negative as well as positive significance: 'God is in heaven, and thou art on earth.' The relation between such a God and such a man, and the relation between such a man and such a God, is for me the theme of the Bible and the essence of philosophy."[1]

## "God Is in Heaven, and You Are on Earth"

This quotation from Ecclesiastes (Eccl. 5:2) gives expression to God's power and superiority over the world by emphasizing God's presence in the heavens.[2] This being of God in the heavens, this primary presence of God in the heavens, evidently makes such a religious impression that being in the heavens, or heavenly being, could be regarded as God's most important, dominant, or even sole characteristic by some biblical texts, many Christian and non-Christian theologies, and all sorts of critiques of religion. God's power over human beings, God's superiority to the world, God's otherness in opposition to all that is creaturely were frequently traced back to God's being in the heavens. At the least they were asserted with regard to God's presence in the heavens. We encounter this emphasis in worship and doxology: "To you I life up my eyes, O you who are enthroned in the heavens!" (Ps. 123:1). Numerous religious traditions and even marginal regions of the biblical canon do not even show qualms about identifying God and heaven. We also encounter the identification of God and heaven in the critique of religion from outside theology, as this critique is formulated by its most important nineteenth-century representatives. It emerges as a critique of heaven, of a world above, of the "beyond." Already the young G. W. F. Hegel demands that the treasures that have been squandered on heaven be brought back to earth. In the nineteenth chapter of Ludwig Feuerbach's *The Essence of Christianity,* we repeatedly find the assertion, characterized as "proof," that "God is heaven; that the two are identical."[3] Feuerbach claims that "the only distinction is, that God is heaven spiritualised, while heaven is God materialised."[4] "In heaven we have stretched into length and breadth what in God is concentrated in one point."[5]

God's power over human beings, God's superiority to the world, God's otherness in opposition to all that is creaturely, *the* difference[6]—even in the theology of this century, all that is traced back to God's being in the heavens asserted with regard to God's presence in the heavens. Statements like those mentioned encounter us with particular force in abstract theological reflections of the early Karl Barth. "Light from above," "movement straight down from above," "new necessity from above," "that which is new from above"—with such formulations, pointing "heavenward," Barth attempts in his famous Tambach lecture to articulate the movement of God's revelation and the foundation of faith's orientation, the foundation of all right theology.[7] God is in heaven: that means that we are to expect God's action, God's engagement in the reality of our lives "from above, straight down from above." "*Depart* from us, you soulish ones, with your interiority. Begone, Satan! That which is beyond, *trans*, precisely *that* is the issue, from that we draw our life."[8]

God is in the heavens. In Christian faith this statement naturally does not claim a fully abstract otherworldliness and an abstract distance on God's part. This statement does not claim this God's total irreconcilability and incompatibility with all earthly, human relations and affairs. Rather the talk of God's being in the heavens is to emphasize and inculcate God's superiority to the world precisely as that superiority can be *known* on earth. The talk of God's being in the heavens is to emphasize and inculcate the dependence of the world and of human beings upon God, as that dependence can be recognized in what is earthly. The talk of God's being in the heavens is to emphasize and inculcate that God and God's action toward the world are not at our disposal and cannot be manipulated. But how?

The early Barth says that in his view the relation of this God to us human beings and the relation of human beings to this God is "the theme of the Bible and the sum of all philosophy wrapped up in one." The phrase "God is in heaven" is intended to register a dialectical relation, a relation of *both* distance *and* relation, of *both* difference *and* engagement. Along the vary same line the Heidelberg Confession says in its interpretation of the invocation of the Our Father: "Why is there added: 'who art in heaven'? (Answer:) That we may have no earthly conception of the heavenly majesty of God [Jer. 23:23f.; Acts 17:24, 25, 27], but that we may expect from his almighty power all things that are needed for body and soul [Rom. 10:12]."[9] Not to think of God's majesty in earthly terms and at the same time to expect from God's omnipotence all that is necessary for both body and soul—can the talk of God's being in the heavens guarantee that? But if God's being in the heavens can in fact register and express God's superiority to the world and the dependence of human beings and of the world upon God, then it is no wonder that the talk of God's presence in the heavens can ultimately stand for the very talk of *God's divinity*. It is no wonder that the talk of God's presence in the heavens becomes an equivalent for the talk of God the Creator and that in the end God and the heavens are even identified. One means God, but one speaks of the heavens. Initially, taking up the Gentiles' outside perspective on the God of Israel, the creator of the heavens and the earth is called in a remarkably abstract and stereotypical manner "God of heaven."[10] The Maccabees letters finally speak of heaven even when God is meant. "The strength that comes from heaven" is invoked. "However heaven wills, so shall it happen." "Let us call upon heaven, that it may be well-disposed towards us and remember the covenant with our ancestors."[11] Human beings cry to heaven. They call upon heaven. They praise and magnify heaven. The texts speak of the grace of heaven, the judgment of heaven and the children of heaven.

Counteracting this problematic tendency to fuse God and the heavens, most biblical traditions carry through significant clarifications and systematizations by emphatically contradicting any divinization of the heavens. The overwhelming majority of biblical traditions and texts unequivocally stress that the heavens are created by God, that the heavens are God's creature. But what sort of remarkable creature are they? Do the heavens perhaps give us occasions and possibilities to determine more exactly what is the character of the creature and creation in general?

## The Heavens—Unity and Plurality of "Transcendence"

The simplest conceptions of the heavens, the conceptions that stand closest to direct sense experience, the most reified conceptions—in the biblical traditions as well—do indeed understand the heavens in the sense of "sky." The heavens are the visible airspace above the earth. Light and darkness, warmth and rain, snow and hail, lightning and thunder come from the heavens. These natural powers from the heavens determine life on earth in a variety of ways. They determine, change, or leave their imprint on both biological and cultural life in many of its forms. At the same time they are not at the disposal of human beings, unlike many cultural powers. Human beings cannot direct them, yet human beings can in the strict sense sensually experience them. The heavens of natural perception can be seen, but they cannot be influenced. They are a realm of creation that in certain respects is "transcendent": they are beyond the active reach of human beings to define and manipulate them. Yet they are not a *numinosum*. For the simple faculty of perception they are vaulted like a bell with the sun, which rises in the east and sets in the west, and thus revolves around the earth. In short, the heavens are exactly as the classic and much-maligned "Astrodome" model abstractly describes it. Alfred North Whitehead concluded that the notorious debates in the "Galileo case" over the correct perception of the heavens, the earth, and the astral world must be revised and readjudicated in light of the knowledge of our day:

> Galileo said that the earth moves and that the sun is fixed; the Inquisition said that the earth is fixed and the sun moves; and Newtonian astronomers, adopting an absolute theory of space, said that both the sun and the earth move. But now we say that any one of these three statements is equally true, provided that you have fixed your sense of "rest" and "motion" in the way required by the statement adopted. At the date of Galileo's controversy with the Inquisition, Galileo's way of stating the facts was, beyond question, the fruitful procedure for the sake of scientific research. But in itself it was not more true than the formulation of the Inquisition. But at that time the modern concepts of relative motion were in nobody's mind; so that the statements were made in ignorance of the qualifications required for their more perfect truth. Yet this question of the motions of the earth and the sun expresses a real fact in the universe; and all sides had got hold of important truths concerning it. But with the knowledge of those times, the truths appeared to be inconsistent.[12]

Galileo was seeking to move beyond the perspective of common sense "underneath the firmament of the heavens." The Inquisition was defending this perspective, which among other things universalizes individual perception. In its rehabilitation of Galileo, the Vatican should have made made these subtleties clear—particularly in a time of often blind trust in the natural sciences' perception of reality.

The biblical perceptions of "the heavens" also go beyond heaven as "sky" and beyond the half-sphere of sense perception. Just as the natural powers of the heavens define natural and cultural life on earth, so also the nonnatural powers that shape natural and cultural life in a way that can hardly be manipulated by human beings are ascribed to "the heavens." Historical and social powers come upon human beings "from heaven."[13] Already in the creation account of the Priestly writing we find highlighted those qualities that distinguish creation from mere nature or mere culture and distinguish the creature "heaven" from a merely natural or merely cultural entity. The Priestly creation account accomplishes this by differentiating the "days" of creation and the days under the heavens, and at the same time highlighting the cultic function of the heavenly bodies, human beings' "mandate of dominion," and the centering of creation on the Sabbath.

Naturally ancient cultures experienced the uncontrollable, dangerous, and threatening as proceeding also from creatures on earth, not to mention from the realm of the sea. But the inevitable and potentially devastating powers came above all from the visible and invisible heavens. One could avoid setting out on the sea, but one could not avoid living underneath the heavens with their uncontrollable possibilities for force. That these heavens are a "creature," however, means that, although they are inaccessible to and uncontrollable by our formative activity, although they are equipped with powers that can decide life and death on earth, they are in principle of the same basic character as the more clearly visible and accessible earth.

A unity thus runs through or overarches all differences of complexity, effectiveness, and power. Reality hangs together with an ultimate homogeneity. The powers that play their dangerous game with us are not in the final analysis totally idiosyncratic. It is a case of something creaturely affecting something creaturely. Moreover, the fact that these heavens—whose powers "from on high" have a happy or devastating effect upon us, whose powers may or may not make sense to us—are themselves a creature means above all that these powers are "in God's hands," as the religious attitude would say. Since the heavens are a "creature," its natural and cultural powers, and the various corresponding instances of transcendence, are subject to God's will, are in principle controlled, and belong—as a secular perspective would put it—to an ultimate association of ordered and interdependent relations, which is in principle accessible to our understanding.

Against this background "God's being in heaven" takes on a totally different quality from that of a "one-upsmanship from above." Instead, God's creatively ruling and ordering action is necessary in order to keep the powers of the realms of transcendence—that is, transcendent relative to the earth—from raging in unforeseeable ways. Thanks to "God's dwelling in heaven," thanks to this creative presence, the powers of heaven cannot possess the bizarreness of hobgoblins or the arbitrariness of fate. In no way does it go without saying that we can assume an association of ordered relations both in what is controllable and in what is uncontrollable, in what is accessible and in what is inaccessible. Suppose we attribute the climatic changes and irregularities of recent years to destructive human interference. It is only possible for us to do so on the basis of assumed regularities and associations of ordered relations that neither we nor the most experienced common sense nor even science has yet sufficiently understood. Assuming these regularities and associations of ordered relations means on the one hand that we do not trust those who, with regard to climatic changes or other irregularities, say, "It's only a coincidence." On the other hand, it means that neither do we trust those who claim that in the long run all that is no problem, in the year 1700 or so it was also hot and stormy, and in the year 2300 and *x* one could experience the same thing.

To be sure, as soon as expectations of regularities have once been unsettled, human beings will no longer exclude what is remote and improbable. Indeed, times of collective insecurity because of the unaccustomed behavior of the "powers of the heavens" are also times in which diffuse anxieties, ancient superstition, and archaic wisdom are again brought to bear in the public arena. But as a rule we expect that even the heavens move and remain within the limits of our experiences. Precisely for that reason we are highly sensitive to considerable or even abruptly appearing departures from the expected pattern. The roots of this sensitivity to irregularities on the basis of a trust in constancy and order lie in the knowledge that even the heavens are a creature—knowledge that in a variety of ways is open to secularization and indeed is secularized. Even the powers of the heavens stand in an association of ordered relations, whether one attributes this association to a divine will or to more abstract, anonymous configurations. In any case the powers of the heavens stand in an association of ordered relations that must be compatible with the creaturely characteristics and conditions that can be perceived on earth and under certain circumstances even has an identical structure and character. The issue here is a trust in relative continuity and homogeneity despite all the instances of difference, uncontrollability, inaccessibility, and transcendence that emerge within what is creaturely, particularly between the heavenly realm and the earthly realm. This trust is not fundamentally shaken when the biblical texts clearly extend the dimensions of their consideration still further.

The heavens that we are able to perceive, the heavens above us that we do perceive, the great Astrodome above us, are limited. Our cultural heavens, our "time and present" with their powers that define us "from above," are also limited. We always live under only a segment of the heavens. More developed perception of the world knows that it can rain on the mountain and be sunny in the valley, that there it is hailing and here it is snowing. More developed experiences even know about the co-presence of heat and frost and day and night on this earth. The natural heavens change not only in their appearance, in the play of their powers and in the threatening exercise of those powers over us. The heavens also change from one perceptual situation to another. The heavens are different over different human beings and landscapes. This is true not only in those regions of the earth that are currently inaccessible and foreign to us or will always remain so. The heavens change in a dramatic manner when we imaginatively assume the perspective of other planets, when we take account of other cosmic systems. One can propose for consideration the question of whether the mixture of pluralization and unification in the designation of the heavens that we encounter in a number of biblical texts is not to be traced back to a consciousness of this state of affairs—whether that consciousness be more or less indistinct or even clearly developed.

Of primary importance is that precisely the trust in the unity and constancy of what is creaturely, despite these evident experiences of discontinuity, difference, and strangeness, makes it possible to assume the unity of the heavens and an ultimate unity of creaturely transcendence. This trust, which is rooted in God's faithfulness, thus allows the heavens to become the foundation and reference point of real universality, which overarches peoples, cultures, climates, and time periods. Whatever may distance and separate the creatures and regions of the earth from one another in time and space, they all have in common that they live under the heavens with their sun, moon, and stars and the orders and rhythms connected with those heavenly bodies. These universal heavens, or in any case these heavens which are conceived as universal relative to the earth, are tied to feats of great abstraction. Nevertheless, we are still dealing with something that can be assumed as a reality in the most straightforward sense of perceptual realities. We have before us not a daring construct or an ethereal idea but a *reality* that appears in countless perceptual contexts and in fact is already incorporated in them, even if always in only a fragmentary manner. The dimensions and complexity of the heavens are overwhelming, yet the heavens can be incorporated by life on this earth in a manner that is adequate, albeit by no means exhaustive.

The creatureliness of the heavens allows us to assume a continuity even in that realm of the world which is inaccessible to us. It allows us to assume a fundamental familiarity with that inaccessible realm, despite the consciousness of a fulness that cannot in principle be calculated, perceived, or measured. According to the biblical creation accounts, the heavens are in tune with the earth, ordered in relation to the earth, created in relation to earthly creatures, human beings, and their perceptual ability. In the Priestly creation account in Genesis we find a disposition to move in this direction. The Priestly account differentiates between two processes. On the one hand is the separation of light from darkness, the separation "in the beginning of the beginning." On the other hand is the creation of the sun, moon, and stars, which themselves separate light from darkness, in the perceptual heavens corresponding to our Astrodome model. The Priestly account sees in a differentiated connection both absolute and relative conceptions of totality—that is, a totality that overarches all perceptions and a totality that is relative to perception.[14]

The biblical traditions are able to go a decisive step beyond the level of incorporating that realm of creation which for us is less determinate and which is inaccessible to our formative activity. They are able to do so because the heavens are a particular location of God's presence. Their particularity consists in the fact that, on the one hand, they form a specific, undeniable sphere of perception while remaining uncontrollable and, on the other hand, they undeniably transcend a single sphere of perception while allowing familiarity. Precisely with regard to the particular character of the heavens and with regard to God's presence in this creaturely realm of power, it is important to recognize and to conceive the interrelation between three characteristics of God's gracious attention: its universality, its powerful concreteness, and the fact that, by the time we "catch up to it," it has also already gone forward, so that we can never encompass or exhaust it. The experience and description of earth in the biblical traditions prove to be scarcely less subtle and striking.

## The Earth—Active and Empowering Environment

The complex constitution of the earth corresponds to the complexity of the heavens. The heavens are a reality that is inaccessible to creaturely formative activity but that nevertheless can perceived with the senses, a reality that is immune to manipulation but that determines life on this earth. The earth is the accessible realm of creation, the realm of creation that shelters life. The image of the house, the *oikos*, has been readily used to characterize the particular character of the earth, especially its orientation toward human beings. Karl Barth offers a catchy formulation: "Because it is dry one can live *on* the earth; because it has been covered with plants one can live *from* the earth. Future creation will be the furnishing of this house as a dwelling. But the twofold work of the third day is that of making the house a *house*."[15] The metaphoric field of the house and household management supplies the grounding for "An Ecological Doctrine of Creation," the striking subtitle of the German edition of Jürgen Moltmann's book on the doctrine of creation. Talk of creation as a "house" is superficially true insofar as creation is thoroughly a matter of creating and furnishing an *environment* that is beneficial to life. More precisely, it is a matter of establishing an interconnection of realms that are environments for each other.[16] Why not designate as "house" an environment that is to be characterized by the expressions "sheltering and supporting" and "trustworthy"?

If, however, we pay careful attention to what happens in the creation account with the creation of life and of things that are living in the strict sense, and with the creation of the creative earth, we see why the expression "house" does not sufficiently define creation in general and the earth in particular. Gen. 1:11-12 and 1:24-25 are the central references to which we should direct our attention here:

> And God said, "Let the earth put forth vegetation, plants yielding seed, and fruit trees bearing fruit in which is their seed, each according to its kind, upon the

earth." And it was so. The earth brought forth vegetation, plants yielding seed according to their own kinds, and trees bearing fruit in which is their seed, each according to its kind. And God saw that it was good. . . . And God said, "Let the earth bring forth living creatures according to their kinds: cattle and creeping things and beasts of the earth according to their kinds." And it was so. And God made the beasts of the earth according to their kinds and the cattle according to their kinds, and everything that creeps upon the ground according to its kind. And God saw that it was good.

Let us initially bracket out the difficult, much-puzzled over difference between God's activity and the earth's activity in Gen. 1:24 and 25: "'Let *the earth* bring forth living creatures'. . . . And *God* made the beasts," etc. Let us concentrate upon the description of plant life and animal life, and of their genesis. Two decisive viewpoints are present and jump to our attention that are not automatically compatible with our standards of thought.

1. The text takes considerable pains in describing the task of the individual species' reproducing themselves. Indeed, the description seems almost picky in its concern for detail. The text also goes to great lengths in presenting the provision of the conditions of the possibility of this individual self-reproduction—conditions that are themselves reproductive. Yet in spite of this involved description of the self-reproduction of the individual species, in spite of the provision of the conditions of the possibility of the individual self-reproduction ("plants yielding seed, and fruit trees bearing fruit in which is their seed, each according to its kind") of what is living, the character of what is living remains, taken in itself, insufficient and secondary with regard to the determination of life. Instead, the primary factor that underlies and precedes these instances of self-reproduction is *the earth*.

As an *environment* that is beneficial to life, that brings forth life, the earth is what is primary. Barth is engaging in a completely typical form of reductionism when he makes this summary statement: "This is life, the living creature, itself produced by God and, without being untrue to its nature, able to reproduce itself in the form of seed, which without being untrue to itself can again be productive."[17] According to the Priestly creation account, it is first the earth that is fundamentally engaged in the activity of bringing forth. As the environment of the plant and animal worlds, the earth brings forth beings that individually reproduce themselves, without again reproducing itself—i.e., the earth—as an individual. This differentiated process of bringing forth demands our attention. It demands our attention if we are

2. to understand why an idea of life that is concentrated upon individualistic self-preservation and self-reproduction is just as mistaken as the determination of the earth as a "house." According to the understanding of the Priestly creation account, the earth is not only a familiar and sheltering envi-

ronment of what is creaturely. It is not only a realm, open to and possessing a determinate shape, of the condition of the possibility of self-preservation and self-reproduction. *The earth is rather an active, empowering agent that brings forth life in the form of various interdependent processes of self-reproduction. At the same time, the earth is to be understood as an environment of various heterogeneous life-processes.* The earth brings forth, but it does not bring forth *itself.* It is not a superplant; it is not a superanimal. The earth brings forth what is creaturely as the latter individually reproduces itself. In doing so the earth is the environment of what it brings forth.[18] It is not merely a receptacle, nor even a well-ordered, well-equipped receptacle. In the particular activity it itself exercises, the earth distinguishes itself from the structure of a house. The earth is an active source of power, an active force field. Without earth's surrounding presence, conveying power, life is not to be thought. From the perspective of the Priestly creation account, we are to call into question conceptions of life that remain fixed upon agents that individually preserve and reproduce themselves.

Odil Hannes Steck has characterized Gen. 1:11-12 as a differentiated description of the phenomenon "of vegetation continually renewing itself."[19] On the basis of the expressions employed by Genesis, the basic conceptual world can be sketched very finely. What is here depicted before our eyes are the "intended appearance of the new verdure," "the fresh growth of every plant," the phenomenon of spring and of young shoots. This process is not understood as due simply to the power and effort of a multiplicity of individuals, as important as polyindividuality and its maintenance and ensurance are ("according to its kind," "according to their kinds"!). Underlying the polyindividual self-reproduction is an empowering environment that in its own manner is engaged in the activity of bringing forth. This environment is the earth. By releasing this power of the earth, God ensures the condition of the possibility of the preservation and constant renewal of vegetable and animal *life.*

We have thus developed and systematically elaborated an understanding that is already present in more rudimentary form in Steck's work, and with the help of which he explains the apparent disparity between Gen. 1:24 and 1:25 ("Let the earth bring forth . . . And God made . . ."). Moreover, this understanding puts an end to the attempts, appearing from time to time in the literature, to solve the riddle of whether the Priestly creation account, whose exposition and judgments are in other respects so differentiated, naively gives an archaic cast to the processes of the generation and birth of land animals ("Let the earth bring forth . . ."). The creation account makes clear that the processes of reproduction deriving from individual living beings, even chains and networks of such processes of reproduction, are insufficient to define and understand "life." But even the conception of environments individually tailored to such processes of reproduction (e.g., the house or houses) blocks our perspective on the powers that lie at the base of life.

On the one hand, knowledge of the character of the earth and its specific life-promoting power pushes us beyond the perspective of the reproduced and self-reproducing individual and beyond the connections that can be and are constructed by that individual. On the other hand, knowledge of the character of the earth and its specific life-promoting power requires correction of even the most developed images and ideas founded upon the metaphoric field of the "house." Knowledge of the character of the earth and of the specific power that it conveys to the creature directs our attention back to difficult theological and religious concepts that as a rule our culture still uses only as (incomprehensible) ciphers—particularly the concept of "blessing." Steck has suggested that the character and power of the earth cannot be grasped with anything less than the fulness of meaning drawn together by the expression "blessing." He takes as his point of departure the observation that according to Genesis 1, God explicitly *blesses* the animals of the sea and of the air, as well as human beings, but not plants or land animals. For land animals, the power of the earth provided by God takes the place of the blessing, functioning as its equivalent. "Here 'Let the earth bring forth' can only mean that the earth, in response to a divine command issued with creation, gives the power that is decisive for the perpetuation of land animals, so that a posterity arises for the land animals . . . . The power that is directed by means of the blessing itself to the animals of the sea and of the air, as well as to human beings, thus lies with the earth with regard to land animals."[20] As Steck makes strikingly clear, it is possible on this basis, on the one hand, to solve the riddle of the difference between Gen. 1:24 and 1:25 and, on the other hand, to understand the hierarchical difference between animals and human beings. The earth in its power to bring forth, the equivalent of the blessing for the animals of the sea and of the air as well as for human beings, ensures the preservation, the vital and enduring population, of plants and land animals. By contrast, God's act of making applies to the initial arising of land animals without the creative cooperation of the earth. Likewise, "in order to highlight the priority of human beings, the perpetuation of land animals is regulated differently from that of human beings." While human beings receive the power for this perpetuation through the blessing directed upon them (blessing as environment!), land animals remain "dependent upon the earth with regard to the power for their perpetuation. The earth has this effect for the land animals on the basis of divine arrangement, while at the same time the earth itself is subject to the dominion of human beings."[21] A grand systematic harmony, confirmed in a variety of perspectives, shows itself in setting up an environment that makes familiarity, the enjoyment of shelter and support, and vital self-reproduction both possible and actual. Such an environment is the earth.

With this knowledge we are still a long way from having exhausted the insights of the biblical traditions into the character of what is creaturely in general, and of "the heavens and the earth" in particular. We have done nothing more than make a beginning at taking with systematic seriousness the fact that "the heavens and the earth" both are and ought to be understood as primary environments of God's presence and of the coexistence of human beings and other creatures. In making that beginning one thing ought to have become very clear. It may be difficult to decode the biblical traditions; it may not be so easy to translate their richly imaginative and figurative language and thought-world into familiar forms of thought. But where this succeeds we can recognize astounding potential for critique of deeply ingrained conceptions and ways of thinking. Precisely if we wish for our understanding to penetrate general concepts such as transcendence, life, and *oikos*, we cannot neglect the critical and inspiring power of the biblical traditions.

# chapter 4
# Angels and God's Presence in Creation

If one looks at God's creative activity, the so-called mandate of dominion, the understanding of creation as heaven and earth, and other parts of the doctrine of creation, it requires no artificial contortions to show that, over against comparable common sense conceptions, in theological questions the biblical traditions are simply more insightful, both in their breadth and in their profundity. But the doctrine of angels seems to land us in difficulties that are utterly insuperable. In a way hardly paralleled by any other object of theological reflection, angels seem to be constructs of pure fantasy that belong to a culture of the past that was not overly precise about truth and reality.

With his characteristic theological imperturbability and sovereign posture of taking the long view, Friedrich Schleiermacher noted in his *The Christian Faith* that the formation of differentiated conceptions of angels belonged primarily to an age "when our knowledge of the forces of nature was very limited." It belonged to an age "when the interdependence of man with nature was not yet settled and he himself was undeveloped."[1] Now one may still make respectful reference to angels only insofar as this underdeveloped knowledge of the powers of nature and the still undeveloped ordering of the connection of human beings with nature are taken into account. (The exceptions are in merely private or in liturgical contexts, where, Schleiermacher is convinced, knowledge of nature and attention to the connection between human beings and nature can be made a matter of indifference.) In the framework of nineteenth-century science, in the framework of any field of knowledge determined by or at least compatible with nineteenth-century natural science, in the framework of any theory of the world possible in Schleiermacher's day, angels are out of the question. The scientific and cosmological displacements of the way in which reality is grasped leave as little room for angels as for the doctrine that the earth is a disc.

In what follows I would not like simply to contradict Schleiermacher. I would not like to maintain that in our contemporary culture angels are compatible with the dominant understandings of reality of either common sense or of more elaborate forms of experience. To be sure, our conceptions of rationality and of reality, and our understanding of science, have changed since Schleiermacher. Indeed, today we are more tolerant toward forms of experience that do not correspond to the dominant ways of acquiring knowledge about the powers of nature. Indeed we have even lost the belief in a homogeneous continuum of rationality and of reality. Yet that does not mean that we are in a position simply to integrate an understanding of angels into our more integrated and more difficult conceptions of reality.

In what follows I would like to draw attention to the problem of mutually incompatible "realities" or views of reality. I would like to do so by attempting to show the high degree of consistency, the high degree of "logical" structure that characterizes the ways in which very diverse traditions hang together that speak about "God's angel" or "God's angels." A doctrine of angels that seeks to grasp the ways in which these traditions hang together is comparable to the forms of mathematical thought for which we do not yet have any realm of application. As Alfred North Whitehead and Bertrand Russell were working on the *Principia Mathematica*, they were astounded at the plethora of theories that emerged which: (1) were consistent within themselves, (2) stood in connection with other theories that clearly provided a guide for experience or were capable of opening up experience, but (3) provided no foreseeable realm of application. Research into talk about God's angels has given rise to similar feelings in me. That research has strengthened my conviction that in a theology that takes its orientation from the biblical traditions, we are never dealing in the long run with purely idiosyncratic thoughts and experiences. We do, however, encounter structural associations of ideas and images that either can no longer be fit into our dominant view of reality and into our forms of experience, or cannot yet be fit again into our dominant view of reality and into our forms of experience. At the same time, although these structural associations of ideas and images cannot be made to "fit in," in their logical consistency they do cast light upon other realms of faith's experience that can readily be brought into connection with our natural experiences. In this indirect way the doctrine of angels illumines God's particular glory, God's particular personality, the particular ways in which God makes contact with what is creaturely, and the particular problems involved in making that contact. I would like to develop this in the following sections.

The first section looks to "God's angel" in "messenger angelology" in presenting the problem of God's withdrawal and finitization of self in the process of making contact with what is earthly and creaturely. The second part explores "God's angel" in "court angelology" to clarify the conception of "God's glory in the heavens."[2] In this we ask, What is characteristic of *God's* revelation—precisely through angels?[3]

## *Messenger Angelology and God's Withdrawal*

Angels mark the particular problem of God's making contact with the creaturely. How can God, whom the heavens cannot contain (1 Kings 8:27; 2 Chron. 2:5 and 6:18), intentionally enter into contact with the creaturely, which cannot correspond to the fulness of God's presence? How can God do this without surrendering God's deity, without becoming unrecognizable in this process of making contact with the creaturely? Dialogical theologies mask this problem by directly appropriating God as a "Thou," as a communicating partner, even if they emphasize the asymmetric and irreversible relation of power between God and creature. Theistic theologies mask the problem by attempting to transpose the process of God's making contact with human beings—a process that has always already occurred—into highly abstract, intellectual epistemic achievements. Or theistic theologies mask the problem by fancying that God is related to everything, to every point of space-time. Mystical theologies mask the problem by dissolving into indeterminacy the determinacy of the process whereby God makes contact.

Several Old Testament traditions repeatedly respond to our question by talking about "Yahweh's angel" or "God's angel." The God whom the heavens cannot contain communicates with the creature, which cannot be everywhere at once, in that God, in God's angel, is attentive to the creaturely. This is by no means the only instance of God's attentiveness to human beings reported by the texts. But it is an instance of attentiveness that is particularly highlighted, particularly interesting, and revealing. It casts light on God's person, on God's way of communicating with creatures, and on God's interest in human beings.

The angel who enters the scene as a messenger of God is to be regarded as a *withdrawal of self*, a *contraction of self*, a *concretion of self* on God's part for the benefit of a revelation to determinate human beings in determinate situations.[4] This is indeed functionally analogous to sending messengers between human beings in a time that did not possess developed technologies of communication. It makes perfect sense that throughout the Old Testament, but also in the New Testament, the expression *mal'ak* or *aggelos* continues to be employed without difficulty for "messenger" in nonreligious contexts.

Human beings can by sending messengers make themselves relatively multiplied. Human beings can through messengers become relatively multi-present. By contrast, when God becomes present in angels it amounts to God's relative finitization or limitation of self. But this self-limitation of God in revelation by means of God's angel is never given fixed form, is never put forward as enduring and repeatable. This perspective is very important, since it is for this reason that it is essential to angels that they disappear and do not return. In the language of our century one could say that angels are existential figures. That is to say that angels are not empirical in the strict sense. As such they cannot be pinned down and measured. The reality of angels is that of a singular event. But the empirical status of singular events remains controverted. If angels are creatures, they are not at any rate to be regarded as *natural* creatures in the usual sense. Although according to the report of the biblical traditions they appear as natural creatures, their reality is more closely related to that of cultural creatures.[5]

I would like to note as a first important point that the angels who appear on the scene as messengers are, contrary to human messengers, not the appearance of a ruler's extension of power. Rather they are the appearance of a contraction of power on God's part. This contraction of God's power needs itself to be retracted, in order not to mask God's presence; the contraction must itself disappear. Second, though, we must attend to the fact that although this contraction of power in God's messenger operates in the midst of creaturely being on earth and operates determinatively upon creaturely being on earth, it does not become an instance of such creaturely being on earth. Angels appear, but they do not take up residence. Angels disappear, but they do not die.

Claus Westermann has characterized angels as "God's possibility for us," saying, "Angels are God's possibilities; they give shape and form to God in his possibilities for us."[6] But this is formulated in too indeterminate a manner. If in angelology one speaks of God's possibility, one must make clear that the angel concretizes and materializes the fulness of God's glory, which we may describe as a fulness of possibilities for determinate human beings in determinate situations. The angel carries through this concretion without masking or negating the fulness of God's glory in this concretion. Westermann puts it nicely: "An angel is . . . God's word or act touching the earth. In one and the same story the narrator can speak of God appearing instead of an angel, and of an angel appearing in place of God, as a way of expressing God's word touching the earth."[7] If we describe this exchange in contemporary theoretical terminology, we can conclude that biblical stories can express by means of an identity switching between God and God's angel this process of God's making Godself present for the good of the creaturely and finite, and under the condition of the creaturely and finite. At issue is a form of presentation that is perhaps imperfect but that in spite of its imperfection is thoroughly appropriate to its material.

Especially in the story of Hagar (Gen. 16) and in the story of Gideon's call (Judg. 6, but also, for example, Judg. 13:22) we encounter this confusing exchange: And God spoke, and the angel spoke. One and the same agent is meant, and yet according to conventional understanding the reference seems to change. Genesis 21, 22, 32, Exodus 2-3, and Num. 20:16, as well as the use of Exodus 3 in Acts 7 also reflect such a double identity.[8] What does this God as angel, this angel as God do?

A group of stories that at first comes across as comparatively fantastic turns out to be revealing for systematic reflection.[9] Balak, a king who is in conflict with Israel, summons Balaam the prophet to pronounce a curse over the Israelite army. Balaam finally sets out on his donkey—initially it is not really clear whether with Yahweh's approval or without it—into the sphere of influence of Israel's opponent. In this situation the angel of the Lord appears on the scene.

> . . . and the angel of the LORD took up a position in the road as his adversary. Now he was riding on the donkey, and his two servants were with him. The donkey saw the angel of the LORD standing in the road, with a drawn sword in the angel's hand; so the donkey turned off the road, and went into the field; and Balaam struck the donkey, to turn it back onto the road. (Num. 22:22-23)

The donkey repeatedly draws back before the angel, but Balaam does not perceive the angel and repeatedly beats the donkey. Thereupon, according to verse 28: "The LORD opened the mouth of the donkey." An otherwise inconceivable linguistic understanding arises between human being and animal. After this understanding between human and animal, verse 31 says: "Then the LORD opened the eyes of Balaam, and he saw the angel of the LORD standing in the road, with drawn sword in hand; and he bowed down, falling on his face." Balaam realizes that his life has been hanging in the balance and that the donkey has saved him. He wishes to turn around immediately, but is sent onward with the commission: "Go . . . but speak only what I tell you to speak" (22:35, cf. v. 20). What is going on here?

With the angel's appearance on the scene boundaries are drawn at the point of transition into a realm of enemy power. At first these boundaries remain thoroughly unrecognizable to human beings. The angel marks the transition into another sphere of power, into the sphere of power of Israel's opponent. At the same time, in connection with the angel's appearance boundaries are removed. Boundaries of communication between creatures are set aside. Almost forty years ago Claus Westermann commented:

> If we look at this story not as enlightened modern men and women who know better about everything, but rather with a readiness to listen, then we will hear something in it that would do our world good to hear. Our mechanized world has little appreciation for animals; we push them to the periphery of our thoughts. But they are creatures, and as such they share in our humanity. We cannot deny them their share without consequence. There is always a point at which animals have a better and sharper alertness than do people. There are moments when it is right and good for people to learn from and heed animals.[10]

What is at stake is not merely learning to be sensitive to animal fellow crea-tures, who—in Westermann's opinion—"have kept their relationship to the Creator even though that relationship is concealed and closed to us."[11] There is more at stake than learning to be sensitive to nonhuman fellow creatures. Admittedly, in situations of ecological danger there is good reason to deplore the absence of such sensitivity. In situations of ecological crisis there are occa-sions when such sensitivity is emphatically demanded. But here something more is going on. The text says that Balaam's eyes were opened. Balaam is given the ability to see in a new way. He is given a new perception of reality. Over against this new perception of reality, the old, accustomed perception of reality, which previously had seemed automatic, is to be regarded as blindness or sleep. Balaam now recognizes a dangerous boundary at this transition into the realm of enemy power. He recognizes a boundary that had not shown itself in the natural view of the natural surroundings. Two processes occur simulta-neously. *On the one hand, boundaries of understanding between what is earthly and creaturely are lifted. On the other hand, there is a sensitization to boundaries and dangers that are not automatically recognizable in the realm of what is earth-ly and creaturely.* Evidently sensitization to boundaries and the lifting of boundaries go hand in hand with the appearing of the angel. Eyes are opened for a view of reality that is both more differentiated and more integrative than is possible with the usual natural and creaturely perception of reality. The nat-ural, unquestioned perception of reality is thereby relativized.

Other texts also present this displacement of boundaries and this calling into question of the so-called natural, accustomed, and routine view of things in connection with the appearance of an angel. But these texts present all that in a way that is considerably less fantastic, considerably less along the lines of a fairy tale, and considerably more normal. In these texts the displacement of boundaries and the calling into question of the routine view of things appear in a way that is considerably more strongly integrated into the world of expe-rience, including into the world of a contemporary common sense. In Joshua 5, Joshua unsuspectingly encounters a man with a sword in his hand. Joshua does not know whether the man be friend or foe.

> Joshua went to him and said to him, "Are you one of us, or one of our adver-saries?" He replied, "Neither; but as commander of the army of the Lord I have now come." And Joshua fell on his face to the earth and worshiped, and he said to him, "What do you command your servant, my lord?" The commander of the army of the Lord said to Joshua, "Remove the sandals from your feet, for the place where you stand is holy." And Joshua did so. (Josh. 5:13-15)

The angel's appearing breaks through and overcomes the militaristic fixa-tion that reality as friend or foe[12] and as corresponding situations of decision.

The appearance of an angel can likewise effectively remove attitudes of powerlessness that have been ingrained by resigned repetition. This is shown, for instance, by the story of Gideon's call in Judges 6. Claus Westermann gives this striking summary:

> In this story from the early history of the Hebrew people, we are told of a farmer's son at work threshing grain, not on the threshing floor but in a winepress that had been hewn out of a narrow depression in the vineyard. He threshed grain there because it was too dangerous to do it out in the open on the threshing floor. You see, the land was under the heel of a conqueror, and had the grain been threshed in the open, occupation troops could—and most likely would—simply confiscate it.
>
> A messenger of God came to Gideon while he was threshing. The messenger was not recognizable as such; in fact, he looked like an ordinary human being. He greeted young Gideon with, "the Lord is with you, you mighty man of valor." Gideon took the greeting literally. . . . Gideon replied in effect, "What does that mean, 'The Lord is with you?' I don't see him. Where are all those mighty deeds he used to do for his people?" The messenger then said that Gideon was destined to be the one through whom those great deeds would begin once again. Quite seriously the young man objected that he was not qualified. Whereupon the messenger answered that it was precisely through Gideon's helplessness that God would accomplish what he intended. Young Gideon listened, yet remained skeptical. He wanted to know who would verify all this, for after all he did not know the angel. Furthermore, he countered, he was just an ordinary person, and the whole thing could be fraud.
>
> At this point we reach the most astonishing part of the story. The messenger accepted the validity of Gideon's objections and gave him a sign to verify the message, a sign that Gideon could recognize. In the act of disappearing the visitor showed himself to be a messenger from the "other" world, and Gideon was able to recognize him for what he was. And what the messenger said would happen did indeed take place. Gideon, now certain that God had called him, gathered a band of men which drove the foe out of the land.[13]

It is important to see that the appearances of angels, as marvelous as they themselves and many of their accompanying circumstances might be, do not in principle change the natural, accustomed view of reality—for example, the accustomed evaluation of relations of political power—so as to sail away on wings of fantasy. Gideon remains realistic, even skeptical. The angel's appearance prompts Gideon to question—as we would say today—what lies behind the formula of greeting and the promise of ways out of the situation. What is improbable and unbelievable in the situation is clearly also submitted to reflection—implicitly by the biblical texts and explicitly by the persons who act in them. Yet the encounter with the angel and the angel's promise then lead to calling into question and changing the situation, including the given political situation. *A new view of reality sets in, which also leads to a change of reality.* Summarizing these first insights, one should note that God's angel appears in the midst of complications and discontinuities in natural relations of life and in natural perceptions of reality, in the midst of menace, betrayal, oppression, and war. God's angel makes possible a relativization and dissolution of the old perception of reality by means of a new perception of reality, which then leads more or less directly to a change of reality.

It is in accordance with this that "the angel of God" also accompanies human beings in situations of permanent danger, in situations of continually uncertain expectations and of continually threatening experiences of difference. The angel accompanies Israel on the way through the wilderness—a way characterized by chronic unpredictability and by continually threatening distress (cf. Exod. 14:19; 23:20, 23; 32:34; 33:2; and Gen. 24). Solidified, persistent menace to the continuity of common life and persistent discontinuous experiences of reality characterize the places where the angel enters into the relations of human, creaturely, and earthly life.

The way in which the appearance of the angel enters into and transforms the perception of reality can be seen most strikingly in the birth announcements to Hagar and to Mary, which are reported in Genesis 16 and Luke 1 (likewise the announcements to Samson's mother in Judges 6). When God's angel promises a pregnancy, this surpasses a woman's experience in a very disconcerting way. If even today a woman's own perception of her pregnancy is initially accompanied by uncertainty, no one in a society without the diagnostic techniques of the twentieth century can leap ahead of this familiarity with self—or a disturbance in one's familiarity with self—in order to know about the coming birth. The angel who has this knowledge thus attains a closeness to the woman that disconcertingly surpasses the woman's familiarity with herself. In announcing a birth, though, the angel not only opens up for the woman a new perception and a change of attitude in inaccessible physical and psychological proximity. The angel also opens up, especially in early societies, a new perception and a change of attitude with respect to socially distant reality lying beyond the reach of influence: that is, with respect to the environment's perspectives on the childless woman. Westermann put it this way: "In a society in which women found fulfillment, honor, recognition, and happiness solely by bearing children, the worst thing that could happen to a woman was to be childless. To give birth to a child after years of waiting, of beseeching, and of disgrace was the most specific and uniquely female experience of deliverance."[14] The angel introduces and even anticipates psychological transformation, a transformation in the relation to oneself but also transformation in the external social perspective on oneself and transformation of regard and of social esteem. The angel of God with his or her improbable message transformatively anticipates experiences of self and reality that are not yet accessible. The angel engages and transforms this world of experience that is near yet inaccessible.

The same holds true analogously for the message of deliverance from political distress in a situation of hopelessness, resignation, and privation. Before the angel's entrance it is simply not foreseeable how the present could be perceived differently than it currently is. It is simply not foreseeable how the future could be looked at other than in indeterminate, passive expectation and continuation of the usual. On the one hand, Westermann has put forward what I consider a dubiously simplifying typology, in which the angel's message responds to the "primal need of woman" and the political "primal need of man."[15] Sabine Grosshennig has called this thesis into question based on the observation that it is their pregnancy that get Hagar and Mary in trouble in the first place. On the other hand, Westermann really does move us forward when he suggests that initially in prehistorical periods questions of family formation and maintenance were the primary questions in giving shape to life and in coping with reality. The familial world functioned as the representative world, the familial orientation as the primary "code" in the perception of reality. Only later did an endangered political structure and reality that continually had to reaffirm itself in armed conflict follow as the primary world, as the representative reality. To be sure, we must give these perceptions and descriptions of reality considerably greater refinement, development, and precision. Yet in any case it is important to observe that the angel's message not only goes out to human individuals in concrete, individual situations. Rather the message in these individual and concrete situations is a message that responds to typical situations of distress and affliction.

Despite the individuality and singularity of the situation, the message of the angel opens up typical, generally relevant perceptions of reality, which at the same time are not readily accessible and not readily changed. The angel makes it possible to see the present that has taken on this fixed form and the future in another way and indeed makes them seen in another way. Private and public self-understanding, private and public perception of reality are changed. According to the biblical traditions, God's angel does *not* appear on the scene *to give purely private revelations*. More precisely, purely private revelations, encounters with an "angel" that remain purely personal and individual, are not encounters with the angel of God.[16]

The biblical traditions provide not only messenger angelology, however, which in its basic constellations is relatively clear. One can also discern in them a court angelology, which at first glance seems to belong to completely different sets of concepts and problems.[17]

## Court Angelology and the Glory of God

For the human being who sends them, messengers make possible a relative multipresence. The effectiveness and realism of this multipresence rise in proportion to the strength of the loyalty that the one who sends the messengers centers upon him- or herself, and in proportion to the number of members who share that loyalty. The ruler who sends out a single messenger to put an army together will presumably have little success. But suppose someone sends out 30 or 300 messengers with the message: "While you, good fellow, are being asked here, 29 or 299 other persons are deciding to defend the fatherland!" That ruler has better chances of winning the numinous "they" or the spirit of the community to the ruler's side and thereby gaining true political power for him- or herself.[18] The Old Testament repeatedly tells of such archaic processes of procuring political power and loyalty.[19]

If we remain within this world of political images, successful, uncontested procurement of power and loyalty is aptly expressed by the picture of the king on his throne surrounded by his court. To be sure, we have here a simple, monocentric image, oriented upon hierarchically divided, stratified societies. But this image, which one can regard as an early, elementary form of political theology, already possesses great conceptual power. This image makes it possible to think God's singular and plural presence, God's determinate and indeterminate presence simultaneously. Moreover, this image makes it possible to imagine the plural presence concentrated, packed together as it were around God's throne. This image of the angelic expression of the fulness and glory of God is developed in at least four ways.

1. The angels around God's throne are *numerous*, indeed too numerous to count. I am indebted to Hartmut Gese for pointing out that a statement like Dan. 7:10: "ten thousand times ten thousand stood before God," meant at that time the largest conceivable number. These angels, who can number in the myriads, can

2. function as *representatives* of peoples, states, epochs, or communities. The expression "collective person," coined by Max Scheler in connection with G. W. F. Hegel's concept of spirit ("an I which is we, and a we which is I"), and taken over and given wide currency by the young Dietrich Bonhoeffer, would be very applicable to angels.[20] Abstractly formulated, angels are themselves to be regarded as personified or instantiated centers of power or of the conferral of religious meaning. These angels, which are too numerous to count and which at the same time each embody a community's power and the foundation of its orientation, are

3. not only present before God, not only attentively centered upon God. In addition, they serve and are ready to serve: that is, they are ready to put themselves at God's disposal, to let God put them into action to serve God's interest. Nor is that all. Angels not only embody potential powers that are at God's disposal, that have placed themselves at God's disposal. A comparison with mercenaries, knights, vassals, or allies would remain inadequate. Unlike the members of earthly armies, the members of the heavenly armies demonstrate and concretize the immeasurable power and glory of God, not by threatening and instilling fear, not by fighting and committing themselves as hungry for victory and prepared to meet death. Instead they demonstrate God's power and glory

4. in *praise of God*, in *doxology*. If we give closer attention to this constellation, it becomes evident that God's glorification is not to be understood simply as recognition and approval. It is also not merely an expression of thanksgiving for a specific act of God or an expression of praise for some specific reason.[21] Doxology goes far beyond specific acts of thanksgiving and praise. In acts of praise and glorification both heavenly and earthly beings point beyond their own perspective on God, beyond their own experiences of God, and thus beyond themselves. This pointing beyond oneself, this relativizing of one's own perspective and experience in the face of God's incalculable glory, is structurally related to the disappearing of the messenger angel! As in assertions of truth we both withdraw ourselves and point beyond ourselves—That is so, even independently of my view!—so doxology points beyond the acquired current, concrete, and personal experience and knowledge of God, beyond all motives at hand for praise and thanksgiving.

Therefore the praise of God is at the same time a summons to praise, as in, for example, Psalm 148:2: "Praise God, all God's angels; praise God, all God's host." Therefore the praise of God goes beyond all spatiotemporal perspectives and realms of experience: "As it was in the beginning, is now and ever shall be, world without end." The angels' praise of God is contagious, expanding and pointing beyond itself. The heavenly doxology of servants of God more numerous than we can take in, who themselves can be regarded as centers and representatives of earthly community and power, reflects the power and glory of God. Paradoxically formulated, in this doxology *the power and glory of God become conceivable even in their inconceivability*. There is a representation of what it means to say: "Even the heavens and the heavens of the heavens cannot contain you" (1 Kings 8:27). The comprehension of the incomprehensibility and incalculability of the divine possibilities for power and glory in the heavens is a fundamental aspect of angelology. To this end the biblical texts employ in their basic structure simple, monocentric forms of political imagery that are quantitatively and dynamically specified along a trajectory that fades into indeterminacy.

Finally, the forms of thought present in messenger and court angelology are maintained in what I consider a consistent manner in the representation of the *individual* figures standing around God's throne, in the representation of the seraphim and cherubim. Westermann comments:

> The winged cherubim and seraphim—mostly in the shape of such animals as lions—go back thousands of years. We find them in a large number of pictures that have come down to us from antiquity. Where they are depicted on temple walls, ritual vessels, or the thrones or statues of deities, they point to the nearness of deity. . . . The seraphim have the appearance of animals, just as do many Egyptian deities, as a reminder of that distant mythical world in which man stood in a relationship between the divine and animal powers which we no longer understand.[22]

Hartmut Gese has spoken of powerful "mixed beings" whom human beings encounter when the latter approach the sanctuary. At the same time Gese has called attention to the fact that these figures cannot simply be dismissed as such merely because they have been taken over from foreign religious or mythical conceptual worlds. Rather we have to consider the representational needs that suggest the adoption of such forms and figures, as well as what it is about the reality in question that gives rise to those needs.

But how can we understand these "angelic figures" theologically? Must we not let matters rest with these critical remarks of Westermann?

> On the one hand, the messengers of God, and on the other, the heavenly creatures of God's court (the seraphim or cherubim, or the forces of nature that serve him) belong to two distinctly different circles of conception. The seraphim and cherubim do not depict two separate troops of a class of creatures that are broadly called angels. That idea came later, when the concept of angels became the predominant concept to which the several kinds of lesser angels then became subordinate. And thus it happened that from Isaiah's description of the winged cherubim and seraphim all angels were thought of as having wings.[23]

Over against Westermann's amicable division into two or three different conceptual circles, it seems important to me to see that the seraphim are *multi-creaturely* figures. Like the need for the appearance of the messenger angels to withdraw (by disappearing), and like the doxological overflow of the court angels, the seraphim also point to a hypercomplex reality, in comparison with which earthly reality represents a reduction. The seraphim embody an association of earthly-creaturely elements that is unthinkable, unimaginable, and impossible under earthly-creaturely conditions, and under the conditions of the world of our experience. Not only are the seraphim, inasmuch as they are endowed with wings and the bodies of lions, superior to human beings in terms of strength and locomotive ability. For human beings, the seraphim are uncanny beings, because they break through the familiar order and typology of what is creaturely and call that order and typology into question. In these beings what is creaturely is joined together in a way that, for human beings, is unknown and neither experienced nor capable of being experienced on earth. The beings who surround God do indeed present recognizable elements of what is creaturely, but they are unlike the creatures found on the earth. They are beings who seem to come from the time in the process of creation before division and determination occurred. In any case the creatures found on earth are poorer in terms of possibilities and power. Some creatures on earth can leap with the strength of the lion; others can fly like birds. But creatures cannot do both.

Over against the power that is expressed in the angels' act of praise, and at the same time relativized with regard to God, all earthly power is only an imperfect level of reduction, indeed a vanishing point. Similarly, all earthly creatures are reduced and deflated figures over against the heavenly beings who directly surround God. The angels in heaven represent a combination of power and reality, an interlacing of reality, a fulness of power and reality, over against which earthly creatureliness, both natural and cultural creatureliness, must appear as a *reduction.*[24] The attempt to perceive these angels in the heavens must lead to overwhelming, incomprehensible images. When individual heavenly beings are nevertheless specified, albeit in improbable form, it must be frightfully uncanny for a human being. Only in doxology can human beings introduce themselves, so to speak, into heavenly relations. Only in doxology can human beings even now anticipate "being like the angels."[25]

In his book on angels, Claus Westermann has pointed out that a clear, new recognition of our dominant, representative experiences of reality, and a clear, new recognition of the experience of elemental distress would have to precede a new sensitization to questions of angelology.[26] Without a clear experience of elemental distress that is typical and representative in a particular time and culture, we will not be able to develop any sensitivity to questions belonging to the doctrine of angels. Westermann warns against appealing to past experiences of distress that today are atypical and uncharacteristic. He warns against using such experiences as a foundation in attempts to thematize representative experiences and to develop a sensitivity to such experiences. It may be that at present global ecological and military crises are pushing us into new, clear experiences of elemental distress and elemental deliverance. Jürgen Moltmann has characterized the culpable entanglement in psychic, social, cultural and natural compulsions as "vicious circles of death."[27] These are cultural mechanisms of compulsion that become autonomous and autonomously extend themselves. All human beings detect these mechanisms, and most persons lament them. Yet like illnesses that are difficult to diagnose or like the dictatorship of the "they," these mechanisms continually elude attempts to interfere with them.

It would be a question for systematic and practical theology whether a doctrine of creation, a theological cosmology, and an angelology could cultivate sensitivity to new, clear experiences of God's salvific intervention in the relations of human life. This is not to claim that our theological undertakings can open eyes that are shut or simply put an end to the sleep of the unquestioned view of the world and of reality. But we can certainly contribute either to distracting from the salvific encounter of what is creaturely with God, or to concentration upon the encounter of earthly reality with God's reality. It seems to me that a minimal presupposition for making a contribution from angelology to a theological concentration of this type is to elaborate the connection between messenger angelology and court angelology in a way that is christologically oriented, realistic in its theology of creation, and systematically consistent. We find such an elaboration at least suggested especially in texts of the New Testament.

It is important to see that in Luke 2 not only is Jesus' birth proclaimed by "an angel of the Lord," but a "multitude of the heavenly host" is present with the angel.[28] Here the heavenly praise of God is connected with the earthly promise of salvation. "Glory in the highest" is announced for God, and peace for human beings. A movement connected with an earthly event also comes into the heavenly court when Luke 5:10 says that there is joy among God's angels over a single sinner who repents. The heavenly host that glorifies God and God's might is tied in a very striking manner to the talk of the "*parousia* of the Human One" to perform judgment, to gather the creatures, and to demonstrate his glory.[29] A systematic angelology would have to attempt to set in relief both the continuities with the court angelology of Old Testament traditions and the shifts in conceptual and imaginative world with regard to the heavenly hosts.[30]

Granted that even if the systematic continuity could be clarified, there would still be no reason to embrace the vision of a prodigious fulness of power belonging to the returning Human One. Admittedly, this vision would be intoxicating enough: Countless angels, who are each to be seen as a concentration and center of power, analogously to the gods and rulers of the nations and epochs, surround the returning Human One and serve him. These angels spur one another on in doxology and continuously transcend themselves and point beyond themselves.[31] As impressive as this arrival of the eschatological reign of God might appear, it would be the task of Christology to make clear both that and why this heavenly host is concentrated, brought into being, and employed in service by the Jesus Christ who became incarnate, was crucified, died, and rose in the flesh. One would need to ask in what way the centering of the angels on *Jesus Christ*, God made manifest, shapes and defines the heavenly hosts' forms of movement and of expression.[32] Only by answering these questions would it be possible to articulate something specific about the eschatological deliverance and transformation of the world, something specific about the eschatological process of God's power and glory becoming public, and thus something specific about the "enduring future of the angels."[33]

But even when the questions are posed in this way, angelology can be of assistance, and can help provide orientation. God's revelation in Jesus Christ seems to fall embarrassingly *below* the level of God's revelation in the angel. It seems embarrassingly not to measure up to the presence of God's angel. God is revealed in God's fulness not in an angel, who by disappearing retracts the divine self-limitation, but in a fleshly, transitory, and mortal human being.[34] Our thinking must honor the connection of the mighty heavenly host—mighty precisely in doxology—with God's revelation in Jesus Christ: incarnate, crucified, risen, and exalted. God is revealed in God's fulness and glory—fulness that cannot be exhausted even by the heavenly hosts in their eternal doxology—in a fleshly, transitory, and mortal human being. "The whole fulness of deity dwells bodily" (Col. 2:9) in this human being, who compared with the heavenly court and the messenger angels is a figure of God's radical, free, and creative self-withdrawal to the point of God's becoming unrecognizeable.

It will not do to assert the presence of the whole fulness of God in Jesus Christ only with regard to Christ's being accompanied by angels. That is, the attempt to define Christ's divinity in terms of angelology will not do. To be sure, angels accompany Christ in the transition to and from this earth. They accompany him in the transition from a reality and to a reality in comparison to which we are to understand this earth as a reduction.[35] It is very difficult, though, to grasp this transition clearly. It is even more difficult clearly to define the place of angels in this transition.[36] Here we must reckon not only with problems of cosmology and of the theology of creation, but also and especially with problems of the clear distinction between angelic and divine presence. Several New Testament texts reflect this complex of problems inasmuch as they give rise to questions about the distinction between the activity of angels and the activity of the Holy Spirit.[37]

Despite these difficulties, which it is impossible to overestimate, it would be wrong to conclude that the inclusion of angelological perspectives makes the theological enterprise more difficult than usual. The angelological perspectives in fact bring new points of view: not only ways of posing problems so as to arrive at new and fertile insights, but also new contours, especially in the relation between the first and second articles of the Creed. These problems and contours not only challenge us to attain clearer knowledge and clearer experience of the glory of God that both has appeared and is still coming upon us. They also help lead us into such knowledge and such experience.

# chapter 5

# Creation, the Image of God, and the Mandate of Dominion

The classic creation accounts of Genesis 1 and 2, which the New Testament traditions also presuppose as setting the standard for the definition of creation,[1] grant to the creation of human beings one of the central positions, if not *the* central position, in the whole process of creation. For a long time this centrality was accepted without question. After all, human beings had apparently been successful in bringing nature "under their control." In any case they tried to persuade each other of this—disregarding irregularities in climatic conditions, earthquakes, volcanic eruptions, insidious germs, and the finitude of their life. In spite of such "remnants of risk," the unquestioned central position of human beings in creation seemed simply to be a fact. It seemed simply to demand recognition, like the rhythm of day and night or the change of seasons. The central position of human beings in the whole process of creation was in any case regarded as a fortunate privilege, or as a distinction—perhaps tied to certain moral responsibilities.

In the last three decades of the twentieth century, two developments above all are destroying this naive anthropocentrism. First, we have begun to recognize that *major ecological crises* jeopardize not only the quality of life of those who enjoy economic and cultural power and privilege. Major ecological crises, caused by the culpable negligence of human beings, now cost countless human beings their lives every day. There is much reason to believe that these major crises could expand into global catastrophes that would make human survival on this earth generally impossible. Second, since approximately two decades ago, sensitivity to the *systematic underprivileging and oppression of women* in our cultures has become a public and political power. The long-standing anthropocentrism of our cultures has become manifest as scarcely veiled androcentrism. Ecological concerns and feminist consciousness have brought to an end the naive or self-satisfied assumption of the preeminent position of "man."

Uncertainty, critical questions, profound skepticism, and protest attach themselves primarily to two complexes of questions and problems:

1. Do not both classical creation accounts support ecological imperialism and vandalism when they ascribe to human beings an absolutely central

and dominant position, consciously defined as dominant? Is it not high time to develop a radical critique of the anthropocentrism of the creation accounts, and of the theologies and doctrines of creation anchored in those accounts?

2. In addtion to ecological imperialism and vandalism, does not the older creation account (Gen. 2:4bff.) in particular support a typically androcentric and patriarchal anthropocentrism by presenting the creation of man and woman and the relation between man and woman as a hierarchy of domination in which the man holds superior place? Is it not high time to develop a radical critique of patriarchal ideology, particularly in the Yahwistic creation account and in the theologies and doctrines of creation rooted in that account? Is it not high time to focus attention on the critique that has already been developed in churches and other public arenas?

In this chapter I examine one area of these critical questions and reservations. Orienting myself on the two classical creation accounts, I attempt to clarify the thorny interconnection between the image of God and the mandate of dominion, the connection between *imago dei* and *dominium terrae* as that to which human beings are ordained. This interconnection has in various ways been theologically glossed over and repressed.

In order to change this, we must first abandon recent theological attempts to use the older creation account of Genesis 2 to relativize the so-called mandate of dominion in the Priestly creation account of Genesis 1. These attempts will be seen to be unconvincing and futile. The second section attempts to provide insight into the complex interconnections envisioned by the classical creation accounts between the image of God, the mandate of dominion, and the sexual differentiation of human beings. It will be seen that representative systematic-theological treatments of the theme *imago dei* (for example, those of Karl Barth and Jürgen Moltmann) sidestep substantive difficulties, albeit in different ways. The third section attempts to clarify both the significance of the mandate of dominion within the framework of the process of creation and the connection between *imago dei* and *dominium terrae*.

## Recent Theological Attempts to Weaken and to Relativize the Mandate of Dominion

For contemporary consciousness, which has become halfway sensitive to the jeopardizing of nature, the problems inherent in the mandate of dominion spring into view at the very first reading of the creation account in Genesis 1. The most important passages are Gen. 1:26, 28 and 29a:

> Then God said, "Let us make humankind in our image, according to our like-
> ness, so that they have dominion over the fish of the sea, and over the birds of
> the air, and over the cattle, and over all the wild animals of the earth, and over
> every creeping thing that creeps upon the earth." . . . God said to them, "Be
> fruitful and multiply, and fill the earth and subdue it; and have dominion over
> the fish of the sea and over the birds of the air and over every living thing that
> moves upon the earth." God said, "See, I have given you every plant yielding
> seed that is upon the face of all the earth, and every tree with seed in its fruit;
> you shall have them for food."

Let us make humankind according to our likeness, and let them have
dominion. Fill the earth and subdue it and have dominion. See, I have given
you every plant and every tree . . . you shall have them for food.—It is difficult not to see human beings conceived and presented here as rulers who do
violence to nature and as consuming possessors of nature. It is difficult not to
find here a theological grounding and justification of René Descartes's famous
history-making phrase—or should we say ideological history-making phrase?
In his *Discourse on Method,* Descartes coined the characterization of
humankind as "*maître et possesseur de la nature.*"[2] Humankind is ordained to
be "master and possessor of nature," and Descartes is convinced that the exact
natural sciences should help human beings live up to this their designation.

The commentaries on Genesis 1 do indeed teach us that both verbs used
here in the biblical text—*rdh* (trample under, subjugate) and *kbs* (subjugate)—belong "in the context of violent subjugation and domination." Both
words for domination are otherwise applied to slaves or to a conquered land.[3]
Although the etymology and translation of both of these expressions have
recently been rendered problematic, the clear parallel passages make dubious
the attempts completely to eliminate from Gen. 1:26 and 28 that in them
which signals the violent use of force. But does this not mean that the creation
of human beings who subjugate the earth and its creatures is the creation of
an existence ordained to assert itself at the expense of others, to overestimate
itself, to endanger both itself and others, and ultimately to be an enemy of creation? How is this compatible with human beings' ordination to be the *imago
dei*? What light do these human beings reflect back upon the God whose likeness they are?

Recent theological discussion has readily contrasted the thorny statements
of the Priestly creation account with a formulation of the older creation
account given in Genesis 2, the so-called Yahwistic creation account. The
Genesis 2 account repeatedly emphasizes that human beings are ordained to
till the ground and precisely so to make possible cultivated vegetation on the
earth. A central passage along this line is Gen. 2:15: "The LORD God took the
man and put him in the garden of Eden to till (*abd*) it and keep (*smr*) it."[4]

To be sure, it is possible to relativize one text by means of the other. In many instances the systematic discussion has proceeded in this relativizing manner, and continues to do so: *Yes,* we find in Genesis 1 the precarious talk of domination, subjugation, and appropriation of the earth and of the creaturely. *But* Genesis 2 breaks this view by making the cultivation of creation, the tilling and preserving of creation, the commission and essential trait of human beings.[5]

What is dubious about this line of argumentation is first the basic problematic of every "yes-but" argumentation. It can be weighted in either the one or the other direction. The argumentation is also dubious inasmuch as Genesis 2, the text that is apparently more friendly from an ecological perspective, exhibits clearer patriarchal motifs than the text of Genesis 1, which apparently formulates an aggressive subjugation of nature as the mandate of dominion, but which emphasizes in an unsurpassable manner the *equality* of man and woman. "God created humankind in the divine image; in the divine image God created them; male and female God created them" (Gen. 1:27)! With regard to the patriarchal problematic, the yes-but see-saw must be reversed in the other direction: *Yes* we find in Genesis 2 a patriarchal subordination of the woman to the man, *but* Genesis 1 speaks in an unsurpassable way about the *equality* of man and woman, inasmuch as the text emphasizes that as man and woman God created humankind in the divine image!

The yes-but argumentation is even more offensive and treacherous, however, indeed much more so. Suppose that Genesis 1 did in fact justify the *maître et possesseur de la nature.* Suppose that Genesis 2 unquestionably offered a religious justification of patriarchal structures. Then, as is familiar to us from past experience, with regard to both problems it would be equally valid for the yes-but argumentation to go in the direction that is currently offensive to most of us. Then it would run: *Yes,* Genesis 1 speaks of an abstract equality between man and woman before God. *But* only the text of Genesis 2 opens up the structural nuances of this equality: first the man, then the woman. The man is the head of the woman, as one can read more or less baldly formulated from Paul to Karl Barth and elsewhere. The unity and equality in question are a unity and an equality that are relativized by their inclusion of hierarchy and subordination. One could argue quite analogously in the other case: *Yes,* Genesis 2 speaks of tilling, preserving, and cultivating as determinations of human behavior toward nature—at least in paradise. *But* it is only the later text of Genesis 1 which honestly and realistically indicates that cultivation always also means subjecting something to one's will, that it means tearing out, cutting and chopping away something that resists cultivation and culture. Genesis 1 owns up to the violence that is still veiled by Genesis 2.

Beside the general problematic of yes-but argumentation, all attempts to relativize the violent anthropocentrism and the strengthening of patriarchy in the creation accounts run into another difficulty. The given division of statements in the two texts *forbids us to relativize along historical lines.* It forbids us to distinguish an original good condition and text from later decline and obfuscation, or to distinguish an incomplete early view from a better, clearer, more developed later one. As things have commonly been understood up till now, those who wish to join the Yahwistic creation account in regarding "tilling and preserving" as the specification of the so-called mandate of dominion must make clear why Paul and Barth, taking equal recourse to Genesis 2, are not historically-exegetically in the right when they connect—whether more or less artificially or not—the unity and equality of man and woman with a hierarchy of domination. Conversely, those who rejoice in the nonhierarchical equality of the sexes that is unquestionably documented in the Priestly creation account must explain why this equality does not strengthen a community of ecological vandals and robber bands composed of both men and women—a community in which contemporary women, at least, would rightly be unhappy to be included.

The texts seem to place us before the unhappy alternative of having to choose between nonpatriarchal partnership bound up with ecological brutality, and ecological circumspection tied to patriarchal structures of domination. Yet are the basic assumptions presupposed in these alternatives correct? Can the exegetical findings and the systematic conclusions, however widespread they might be, be regarded as tenable and on the mark? From the numerous approaches that are possible and necessary for clarification, I have selected one: namely, the approach by way of the question of the mandate of dominion.[6]

## *The Image of God, the Mandate of Dominion, and Sexual Differentiation of Humans*

Every attempt to clarify and to understand the manifold connections between the unquestionable anthropocentrism of Genesis 1, the designation of human beings as being in the image of God, the so-called mandate of dominion, and the relation of man and woman, runs into a whole series of difficulties.

1. Does the image of God refer to the relation of created humankind as male and female? Gen. 1:27 would argue for an affirmative answer: "So God created humankind in the divine image . . . male and female God created them."

2. Or does the image of God refer to the so-called mandate of dominion? Gen. 1:26 would argue for an affirmative response: "Then God said, 'Let us make humankind in our image, according to our likeness, so that they have dominion over the fish of the sea, and over the birds of the air, and over the cattle, and over all the wild animals of the earth, and over every creeping thing that creeps upon the earth.'"

3. Or does the image of God finally refer to the connection of both aspects, the connection of the relation of man and woman with the mandate of dominion? Gen. 1:28 would argue for an affirmative answer: "God blessed them, and God said to them, 'Be fruitful and multiply, and fill the earth and subdue it; and have dominion over the fish of the sea and over the birds of the air and over every living thing that moves upon the earth.'" To what does the image of God refer?

If the image of God referred to the relation between man and woman, the interpretation could abstract from the whole aspect of *violent* anthropocentrism. Along with Karl Barth[7] and interpretations similar to his, an interpretation could concentrate upon the aspect of *partnership*. According to Barth, "the analogy between God and man . . . is simply the existence of the I and the Thou in confrontation."[8] Barth is convinced that this face to face existence of I and Thou is "first constitutive for God, and then for man created by God. To remove it is tantamount to removing the divine from God as well as the human from man."[9]

In view of Barth's dominant interest in partnership in general, and specifically in the I-Thou constellation, he gives a remarkably short treatment to the explicit emphasis upon sexual differentiation in the Priestly creation account. Barth initially emphasizes that with sexual differentiation something is emphasized that human beings have "formally . . . in common with the beasts." He adds the interesting reflection that human beings are distinguished from animals precisely inasmuch as "in the case of man the differentiation of sex is the only differentiation. Man is not said to be created or to exist in groups and species, in races and peoples, etc. The only real differentiation and relationship is that of man to man, and in its original and most concrete form of man to woman and woman to man."[10] But Barth does not go beyond the emphasis upon the formal likeness with animals and beyond the exclusion of racial, ethnic, and other supposed "differentiations of creation." Primarily interested in, indeed as good as fixated upon the abstract partnership in the I-Thou relation, Barth does mention "the peculiar dignity ascribed to the sex relationship."[11] He also emphasizes that "in all His future utterances and actions God will acknowledge that He has created man male and female, and in this way in His own image and likeness."[12] Yet then follows with an astounding abruptness: "But these are matters which are more explicitly treated by the second biblical witness, and we will not anticipate their development at this point."[13]

In this place and in the perspective that is relevant here, Barth does not wrest further insights from the Priestly creation account than the I-Thou relation, the formal likeness to the animals, and the exclusion of basic anthropological differentiations other than the sexual one. For the more exact determination of the relation of man and woman, and for the specification of the ordination to the image of God, Barth refers us to the Yahwistic creation account, which, as is well known, Barth interprets more or less subtly along the line of the patriarchal conception of hierarchy.[14]

Jürgen Moltmann likewise wishes to connect the image of God to the relationship between human beings, and not to the mandate of dominion.[15] To be sure, he wishes to avoid the personalistic concentration on the I-Thou relation that ruled all of Dialectical Theology (such as Karl Barth's), as well as the reference to a relation of hierarchical dependency. Moltmann assembles a series of observations on the particular interlacing of plurality and singularity in God and human beings in order to arrive at an understanding of the image of God as unity in community.[16] Moltmann holds that a pluriform community of human beings corresponds to "the God who is in his very self community and a wealth of different relationships."[17] He elaborates:

> In human likeness to God, the analogy is to be found in the differentiation in relationship, and the wealth of relationship in the differentiation. It is this which, in the triune God, constitutes the eternal life of the Father, the Son and the Spirit, and among human beings determines the temporal life of women and men, parents and children. This socially open companionship between people is the form of life which corresponds to God.[18]

In this way Moltmann wants to mediate his interpretation of the image of God with what he calls the "social doctrine of the Trinity," which attempts to comprehend the triune God as a perichoretic communion.[19] Moltmann of course concedes that the Priestly creation account does not develop a full-fledged doctrine of the Trinity. But he does think that the Priestly account is open to such a doctrine.[20] Fundamental for this understanding is, according to Moltmann's interpretation, the interlacing of the plural of deliberation and the singular: "Let us (plural) make humankind in our image (singular)" (Gen. 1:26) and "male and female (plural) God (singular) created them" (Gen. 1:27). Moltmann comments: "The image of God (singular) is supposed to correspond to the 'internal' plural of God, and yet be a *single* image." In the opposite direction, the "human plural" indicated by means of sexual differentiation is supposed "to correspond to the divine singular."[21]

Like Barth, Moltmann's emphasis on sociality and sociability as the root and form of the image of God abstracts from essential statements of the Priestly creation account. Moltmann does indeed repeatedly highlight the fact that "at the creation of human beings, the division into two sexes is particularly mentioned." It is in the sexual relationship that "the real likeness to God and the uniquely human quality must lie."[22] But then Moltmann—in a way that is formally comparable to Barth's abstract I-Thou model—grasps the sexual relation in the abstract and sublimated form of sociality and sociability. Without advancing any supporting reasons, he claims that the sexual relation is "not tied to fertility."[23] With a similar absence of any supporting reasons, Moltmann separates the "social" image of God from the mandates of dominion:

> The creation of God's image on earth is followed in v. 28 by the commission to rule over the animals, and in vv. 28 and 29 by the charge to "subdue the earth." These commissions are not identical with the likeness to God; they are a specific addition to it. This means that the likeness to God is not, either, to be found essentially in these commissions to rule.[24]

Over against models of I-Thou partnership (Barth)—whether they are conceived in an egalitarian manner or with reference to patriarchal hierarchy—and over against the model of universal sociality and sociability (Moltmann), Phyllis Bird has developed a third model. In an in-depth investigation of Cen. 1:27b ("in the divine image God created them [humankind], male and female [God created them]"), Bird has urged us to see that precisely sexual differentiation and biological reproduction are the decisive viewpoint of the partnership and image of God focused upon by the Priestly creation account. Summing up her argument in a way that consciously drives home her point, Bird says that Gen. 1:27 describes the *biological couple*, not a merely social partnership.[25] She supports her thesis with recourse to the general anthropology of the Priestly writings (P), which she argues are strongly androcentric because they compose the genealogies and the establishment of the cult, which is so important to the Priestly writings, in a thoroughly androcentric manner. Bird holds that Gen. 1:27 is compatible with this only if the verse could be understood as a screening out of cultural and social perspectives and could be restricted entirely to the biological function.

The egalitarian statements are incompatible with the basic posture of androcentrism that can be observed in the rest of the Priestly writings. Therefore the emphasis upon the community of man and woman can only be a matter of highlighting the capacity for biological reproduction. To be sure, Bird concedes that, in the history of interpretation and in what systematic theology can make of this text, the text's approach points beyond the androcentric conception of the Priestly writings and beyond patriarchal structures of hierarchy. For from then on, both man and woman had to be recognized as characterized by the image of God. The "natural" parameters established by creation thus offer no basis for the hierarchical differentiation or devaluation of the image of God, defined as both masculine and feminine. Bird sums up her findings thus: "Contemporary insistence that woman images the divine as fully as man and that she is consequently as essential as he to an understanding of humanity as God's special sign or representative in the world is exegetically sound even if it exceeds what the Priestly writer intended to say or was able to conceive. Like Paul's affirmation that in Christ there is no more 'male and female' (Gal. 3:28), the full content and implications of the Priestly statement lie beyond the author's ability to comprehend."[26]

The great strengths and advantages of the approach chosen by Bird include not only the ability to accord systematic seriousness to the text's emphasis on sexual differentiation. In the models of partnership, sociality, and sociability, this emphasis is submerged, despite assertions to the contrary. Over against a recourse to abstract I-Thou partnership or general sociality and sociability, Bird's hold on the biologically tangible differentiation is striking. But the greatest advantage of Bird's approach is its ability to connect the presentation of the image of God as man and woman with the so-called mandate of dominion: that is, its ability to delineate this connection in the text. Bird is not compelled to let Gen. 1:26 fall apart and to let Gen. 1:27 and 28 go their separate ways. With Gen. 1:28 one can on this basis emphasize that both being fruitful and multiplying, on the one hand, and subduing the earth and having dominion over it, on the other hand, stand in close connection to each other. Moreover, this corresponds to the statement of Gen. 1:26: "Let us make humankind in our image, according to our likeness, so that they have dominion . . . ."

In comparison to Bird's understanding, the partnership and sociality models of Barth and Moltmann convey a certain abstract harmlessness. The image of God is not simply human beings in dialogue or in plural sociability. The image of God is men and women who exercise domination as they multiply and spread over this earth. Of course, they can also behave in relation to each other in ways that are dialogical and socially open.

Accordingly, Bird gives sober emphasis to the imperial constitution of the exercise of this mandate of dominion. She unequivocally presents *rdh* and *kbs* as activities of subjugation and subordination. "If there is also a message of responsibility here, it is not dependent on the content of the verb but on the action of God in setting *adam* over the creatures in an ordered and sustaining world."[27]

Although Bird's approach is closer to the text and does greater justice to its subject matter than do the dialogue and sociability models, it also is not completely convincing. The difficulty lies in her insistence that *only* the biological couple and *only* biological reproduction are intended here. As the first chapter of this book demonstrated, our dichotomization of "nature" and "culture" is foreign to the classical creation accounts. On the contrary, so-called natural and so-called cultural factors are seen very subtly in indissoluble reciprocal connections. A merely physical reproduction of human beings would not even be adequate to fulfill the mandate of dominion, especially since we must not presuppose the contemporary situation of our world with its human overpopulation and its exploited and exhausted natural environments as the biblical traditions' system of reference.

If Bird's interpretation were linked to the insight that, with regard to humankind, biological reproduction *and* cultural development are necessarily connected, her interpretation could encompass the elements of truth in Barth's and Moltmann's interpretations. And it could do so without surrendering its own correct and superior insight that in Genesis 1 biological reproduction, equality of the sexes, and powerful domination are indissolubly connected. Human beings become so powerful precisely because they connect biological reproduction and cultural development. The contemporary situation of our world confirms that they become powerless where this connection is in one way or another surrendered.

If we do not read Genesis 1 selectively but attempt instead to attach equal weight to all its statements, the text compels us to the insight that the image of God is not merely human beings as dialogue partners or as plural participants in open communication. According to Genesis 1, the image of God is men and women who exercise domination as they multiply and spread over this earth. But why does this sober image not simply leave us horrified? Can we on this basis still wrest any meaning, any positive characteristic from the so-called mandate of dominion? Is the connection between *imago dei* and *dominium terrae* in Genesis 1 about nothing other than the sad and brutal truth of the human species, which asserts its strength to prevail biologically and culturally? If this were indeed the message of the creation account in Genesis 1, to what extent does this power-centered and violent anthropocentrism not rebound in a negative, sobering, or distorting manner upon the image of God and upon God's own self? To what extent does not the mandate "Subjugate the earth and rule over the animals" completely compromise everything that may be found and envisioned in the notion of the image of God in terms of partnership, sociality, sociability, and solidarity among human beings?

## The Mandate of Dominion: Obligation to Hierarchically Ordered Partnership with Animals and to Dominion through Caretaking

In an important and much-noted article with the title "Shape the Earth but Tend Life: Several Clarifications Concerning *Dominium Terrae* in Gen. 1,"[28] Klaus Koch, taking up ideas of Norbert Lohfink,[29] has made clear that in this passage the expression *rdh* "refuses to be fit into the straitjacket of 'trample under' that the exegetes clap over the text." According to Koch, *rdh* has to do with the "guiding, pasturing, fostering behavior of human beings towards animals." It is a question of "the particular achievement of the first among equals."[30] Yet how do we bring together the meaning of *rdh*, which in any case applies to the domination of slaves and foreign peoples, with the meaning emphasized by Koch?

Gen. 1:30, a verse that normally receives little attention in the context of the question we are posing, offers a key that is at first glance wholly unremarkable. Gen. 1:29 reads: "God said: 'See, I have given you every plant yielding seed that is upon the face of all the earth, and every tree with seed in its fruit; you shall have them for food.'" Then follows Gen. 1:30: "'And to every beast of the earth, and to every bird of the air, and to everything that creeps on the earth, everything that has the breath of life, I have given every green plant for food.' And it was so."

Let us begin by looking back from Gen. 1:30 with the vision of the vegetarian community of solidarity between human beings and animals. The ordinance in Genesis 1 that both human beings and animals are to nourish themselves as vegetarians is not the subject of exegetical controversy, and most systematic expositions also simply accept it at face value. In the present exposition we will not delve further into the contents of this ordinance. We will concentrate solely on the ordinance placing human beings and animals in a community of solidarity and on the resultant problems. What does this mean? Both human beings and animals are to take their nourishment from the plants that sprout on the surface of the whole earth. Human beings and animals thus have a common realm of life and nourishment. One can already envision problems, tensions, colliding interests. How will conflicts of interest between human beings and animals be regulated? How should human beings behave when animals, in their interest in nourishment, drive humans away from plants yielding seed? How should animals behave toward human beings, when human beings use the plants yielding seed for their own nourishment? It is at this point that the situation necessitates the so-called mandate of dominion.[31]

The mandate of dominion serves to impart a differentiated order to the "world of nourishment" shared by human beings and animals. This order is established through a hierarchy of power. On the one hand, human beings and animals are neighbors and live together in a common sphere. On the other hand it is clear and unequivocal that animals—analogously to slaves and to subjugated peoples—are living beings secondary and subordinate to humankind. There is no question of allowing one's neighbor to starve in favor of one's housepet. Human beings have primacy over animals. The vocabulary is unequivocal inasmuch as the ordering is anthropocentric. In no case may an animal be given higher status than a human being. That is radically excluded. At the same time there is a community of nourishment and of interests between human beings and animals. Just as the admittedly lesser rights of slaves are secured in the Old Testament bodies of law, and just as the subjugation of foreign peoples can extend to taking them into service but not to exterminating them,[32] so the relation of human beings to animals is a relation of tolerance and of preservation in human beings' own interest, indeed in what is most deeply their own interest.

The mandate of dominion provides for an unquestionably one-sided and hierarchical relation between humans and animals. We should not cultivate romantic images about this relation. At the same time this unquestionably violent relation must not be a relation involving brutal or indifferent extermination. Instead it is positively determined in a twofold manner. First, it is God's will that human beings stand in a community of solidarity with animals. They stand in a community of solidarity not only inasmuch as they increase their population analogously to animals (Barth), but also inasmuch as they are supposed to live with animals of the earth and air in a common realm of nourishment. Second, as "God's image" human beings stand over against animals.

Human beings extend God's solidarity and care to what is creaturely. They do so in a manner that is decidedly diminished, that presents only an image, that is, only a likeness. They extend God's solidarity and care in spite of their mighty self-reproduction and self-extension. They extend God's solidarity and care in spite of the overwhelming way in which they fill the earth. They extend God's solidarity and care in spite of their designated domination over other creatures. The fact that they are supposed to have "dominion" over the animals thus also means—definitely based on royal ideologies of the Ancient Near East—that they must exercise responsibility toward animals. As rulers over animals, human beings must grant animals a relative level of "rights." "In the face of rival demands and interests," human beings have the function "of serving as judge[s]."[33] Over against animals, who are subordinate to them, human beings must practice "mercy," that is, the systematic protection of those who are weaker.[34]

In an attempt to highlight the decisive difference between this mandate of dominion and the modern understanding of the "mastery of nature," Erich Zenger has emphasized that human beings are not summoned to exercise dominion "in the sense of modernity's well-known triumphalistic anthropology." Instead they are made "royal deputies of God the Creator."[35] Bernd Janowski has further developed this perspective in a careful investigation that supplies abundant material on the topic.[36] Janowski has proposed using the "metaphor of the 'royal human being'" to comprehend the connection between the image of God and the mandate of dominion. Janowski is encouraged to take this position both by royal ideologies of the Ancient Near East and by the recognition that humankind is supposed to exercise dominion not only over land animals, but also over fish and birds and thus over all living beings in all regions of the earth. This task extends beyond humankind's directly looking out for its own interests. Odil Hannes Steck sheds light on this task specifically with regard to Noah's behavior:

> The measures which Noah takes, at God's command[!] . . . to secure the survival of the animal world during the Flood are certainly seen by *P* as the practical exercise of man's task as ruler. The purpose of preserving the life of the endangered animal world, which is expressly stated in [Gen.] 6:19, 20 is highly significant. Just as man himself belongs to the natural world of creation, in that he lives and carries on his life in the world, so his divine stewardship expresses itself precisely in the fact that he has to preserve the right to live and the contribution to life of the natural world and environment as a whole. That is to say, he has to preserve the right to life of living things apart from himself as well.[37]

If we attend to this connection between protective dominion and self-preservation or self-reproduction, and if we attend no less to the fact that the mandate is given to the "royal human being" as a couple, as man and woman, the result is an image that is fruitful precisely in its tension: Evidently human beings in their correspondence to God are to be "fatherly and motherly" in their "royal" comportment, and in their motherly and fatherly behavior they are to realize a royal existence! The exercise of dominion is qualified by caretaking, and caretaking is qualified by dominion.

The mandate of dominion does not ordain human beings to a community of solidarity with animals that would make it possible to confuse children and housepets, human beings from other lands and exotic animals. Precisely the proximity to animals, precisely the insistence that human beings and land animals share a common sphere of life, makes it important to emphasize the contrary view! Conversely, the exercise of dominion not only is limited, its orientation is that of "dominion by caretaking"—despite the specification of characteristics that include the use of force. The relation in question does indeed provide for the use of force, and there is indeed a hierarchical gradation within the community of solidarity and nourishment. But the use of force must not destroy this community. Humankind, created in God's image, must cultivate this community and preserve it in a specific form, namely, one that bears responsibility for those who are weaker. Despite the fact that human beings look out for their own interests over against animals and act to secure those interests, the use of force is shaped and limited not only by the community of solidarity itself and by its requirements for preservation but also by the mandate to represent God's image. Indeed, as Klaus Koch observes, part of humankind's *rdh* is "to care for the nourishment of animals and to secure their living space. The sense of this arrangement is especially obvious in the Middle East, because the opposite of cultivated land is not wilderness, but desert."[38]

The mandate of dominion aims at nothing less than preserving creation while recognizing and giving pride of place to the interests of human beings. In all the recognizing and privileging of the interests of human beings, the central issue is the preservation of creation in its complex structures of interdependence. The expansion of the human race upon the earth is inseparable from the preservation of the community of solidarity with animals in particular, and inseparable from the caretaking preservation of the community of solidarity with all creatures in general. God judges human beings worthy of this preservation of creation. They are to exercise dominion over creatures by protecting them. Human beings acquire their power and their worth precisely in the process of caretaking. The mandate of dominion according to Genesis 1 means nothing more and nothing less.

This clarification is not rendered less important by the fact that the Bible certainly develops other perspectives on the relation between human beings and animals.[39] It is not rendered less important by the fact that—in a different context—the problems resulting from the mighty self-reproduction of human beings are seen clearly,[40] indeed that human beings ignore and misuse the mandate of dominion, and that the *imago dei* gets lost under the power of sin. These problems push us into new territory, but they do nothing to change the clear connection between the image of God and the mandate of dominion, rightly understood.

# chapter 6
# Creation and Sin

"What do we mean by 'God'? Not in the first place an abstract belief in God's omnipotence, etc. That is not a genuine experience of God, but an extension of the world."[1] This idea, formulated by Dietrich Bonhoeffer in the last months of his life in the sketch of a planned writing, needs to be refined on the basis of the insights worked out earlier in this book. Images and ideas of God as abstract, undifferentiated ideas of omnipotence are not simply "an extension of the world." They are an extension of the world perceived in the absence of spirit and without bearing witness! Images and ideas of God as abstract, undifferentiated ideas of omnipotence are an extension of the world *not perceived as creation.* The abstract idea of omnipotence ignores the sensitivity of faith for relations of power, relations of powerlessness, and the manifold ways in which the two are interlaced. Busy with its speculations, it misses the creator and the creation.

Where do the abstract idea of omnipotence and other primitive conceptions of power find their foundation and support? Anyone who wishes to answer this question must focus upon the difficult connection between *creation* and *sin.* Under the power of sin human beings not only proliferate disruption, dissociation, and destruction. Under the power of sin human beings also generate the illusion—indeed in connection with sin's devastating activity—that they possess great oversight and clarity, or indeed that they have great power to steer and direct both secular and religious matters. In this situation human beings are strangely helpless.[2] I would like to clarify this part of the constitution of human existence with reference to Genesis 3, particularly Gen. 3:22. In doing so I am conscious that I am picking out only *one* aspect of the complex connection between creation and sin.

## *"The Fall" or the Autonomy of Created Humankind?*

At first glance Gen. 3:22 has nothing to do with "sin." For G. W. F. Hegel and for representatives of so-called left-wing Hegelianism, who are as a rule well-acquainted with the biblical traditions, Gen. 3:22a instead gives witness and religious confirmation to the source and content of humankind's autonomy. "Then the LORD God said, 'See, the human being has become like one of us, knowing good and evil [what is beneficial to life and what is detrimental to life].'"

There is no other word of Scripture that the mature Hegel cited as frequently as Gen. 3:22a.[3] The indirect references to Gen. 3:22, and to Genesis 3 in general, are innumerable. Hegel explicated the program and fundamental ideas of his philosophy with regard to Gen. 3:22a. In one of those places, in a review of the writings left behind by Solger at the latter's death,[4] Hegel emphasizes that *one* "moment" of creation contains "not only the source of evil, the act of eating from the tree of the *knowledge* of good and evil, and thereby of *falling away* from the image of God . . . but also the principle of the return to that image." Hegel adds that in this text "God's own self is introduced as speaking: See, Adam has become like *one of us* and *knows* what is good and evil (1 Moses 3:22)—the passage that constitutes the other side to the first meaning of that knowing, and which customarily is far too seldom treated in its depth, indeed even considered."[5]

If we untangle Hegel's difficult diction somewhat, his position runs as follows. To creation belongs not only the fall from the image of God and thus the "source of evil." To the extent that this fall is bound up with the *knowledge* of good and evil, the "principle of the return to that image" is also anchored in the event of creation, which Hegel conceives in a correspondingly broad manner. There is much to be said for the argument that when Hegel voices the reproach that Gen. 3:22a is "customarily far too seldom treated in its depth," he has in view a tradition of interpretation that cannot hasten too quickly to put forward the assurance that this text is irony and sarcasm. "*Est sarcasmus et acerbissima irrisio,*" in the words of Martin Luther's lectures on Genesis (published 1544–54).[6] Likewise John Calvin's interpretation of Genesis (1554) describes the text as "an ironical reproof, by which God would not only prick the heart of man, but pierce it through and through."[7] Calvin sees himself compelled to explain why God "does not, however, cruelly triumph over the miserable and afflicted," and Calvin tries to refute the view that also takes 3:22b "to be an irony."[8]

The Neomarxism of our century, influenced as it is by left-wing Hegelianism, has concerned itself with seeing to it that Hegel's theory of the connection between the fall, the acquisition of autonomy and the return to the *imago dei* does not recede into oblivion.[9] In his writing on "Atheism in Christianity," Ernst Bloch poses the provocative question: "Is not knowledge of good and evil the very same as becoming a man?—as leaving the garden of beasts, where Adam and Eve still belonged? . . . But precisely in this passage, the most outstanding passage in the whole of the 'underground' Bible, the glint of freedom is ill-concealed."[10] The fall as the true process of becoming human, as the splendid acquisition of freedom, and this acquisition of freedom as the severing of ties with the garden of animals! Bloch repeats in his own way what Hegel saw and said. Bloch ascribes it to the "other Bible": the subversive, emancipatory Bible, with its focus on freedom, or the corresponding layers of the biblical traditions. Freedom, autonomy, return to the *imago* instead of the fall and sin! Did not God's own self say: "See, the human being has become like one of us, knowing good and evil"?

Whether following in Hegel's footsteps or not, it is noteworthy and astounding that since the talk about God's irony has grown silent, recent Old Testament research sees central concepts of anthropology, epistemology and ethics anchored in this passage. Looking at Gen. 3:22, exegetical research talks about the source of "reason,"[11] of "consciousness,"[12] or of "autonomy" and "self-determination."[13] Underlying the choice of these concepts stand at least:

1. the expression "knowing good and evil"
2. the statement "See, the human being has become like one of us"

How are we to understand both these statements and their interconnection with reference to Genesis 3?

The very attempt to say what is meant by "knowing good and evil" enables one to recognize that Gen. 3:22 places high demands upon theological reflection. If one examines the commentaries on the passage, one sees that Claus Westermann has drawn his orientation from subtle and differentiated attention to the expression's fields of meaning within the traditions of the Old Testament. On that basis he has stated the minimal requirements that are to be made of any attempt to elucidate the expression "knowing good and evil," where that attempt is really concerned to think with Scripture and not to introduce external reflections.[14]

The expression "knowing good and evil" is

1. "to be understood as a whole . . . [so that it] describes a particular way of knowing."[15] At issue is a unitary manner of orientation, not mere acts of knowing some particular good thing or some particular evil thing.

2. This knowing is related to something that is "good or evil for humans": that is, is beneficial or detrimental to life. What is in question is not mere cognitive perception, but an active, determinative, conclusive "distinguishing the useful and the injurious."

"Knowing good and evil" is a unitary theoretical *and* practical orientational behavior. By taking note of and conclusively distinguishing what is beneficial and what is detrimental, this behavior makes it possible, in Westermann's formulation, to "succeed" "in the context of the struggle for existence."[16]

3. This behavior "should not be understood—or at least not merely understood—as the function of an individual or something that happens to an individual." Its subject "is really humankind in its origination." It is a behavior and a process "which is directed to the life of the community and which reaches its fulfillment in it."[17]

If one attempts to connect even some of these presuppositions in a way that attaches equal importance to each, it may seem impossible to overcome the difficulties in indicating what "knowing good and evil" really means. But these presuppositions provide the basis for explaining both why the source of consciousness or of autonomy and self-determination was seen here, and why these typically modern views are too narrow.

First, if *lada`at* is emphasized, this could suggest speaking of consciousness (Gese) and understanding the so-called fall as the genesis of conscious human perception of reality. A realm of diverse epistemic functions would be named that would also be able to take account of the unity of polar (or contrary)[18] opposites (good and evil). But this approach would not yet have grasped the essentially practical character of the knowledge of what is beneficial to life and what is detrimental to life.

Further, one might point out that, in consideration of the expression as a whole—emphasizing the unity of its elements—the practical function of this knowing would have to receive stronger expression. If one does so, the concepts of autonomy and self-determination present themselves (Steck). The "creative act of the determination and specification of something that is beneficial and harmful to life"[19] can then stand center-stage. It seems that epistemic processes, discernment, decision and specification can be bound together in this act.

Yet both of the proposals mentioned are strongly oriented on the human individual and her or his epistemic faculty, or alternatively on elementary individual epistemic achievements. The first proposal fixes a comprehensive realm of intellectual behavior, the second, a central act that points beyond intellectual behavior. But both proposals do not attend sufficiently to the remark that "knowing good and evil" "should not be understood—or at least not merely understood—as the function of an individual or something that happens to an individual." Instead we are to attend to a "function of humankind in its origination"—an origination that finds its fulfillment in the "life of the community" and is related to that life![20]

How can we define the expression "knowing good and evil" in a way that transcends the overly narrow (because centered on the individual) concepts of consciousness and of autonomy or self-determination? We ought to speak of a *fundamental ordering event, an ordering behavior aimed at the organization of the realm of human life with regard to what is beneficial and detrimental to that life.* With regard to the individual determination of something as beneficial or harmful to life, we could speak of autonomy. With regard to the individual epistemic realm that encompasses what is beneficial and what is harmful, we could speak of consciousness.

This talk of an ordering behavior or an ordering event aimed at the organization of the realm of human life with regard to what is beneficial and detrimental to that life could certainly be given further fruitful precision from the perspective of Hebrew thought. Such talk points to the self-directing power of humanity as it observes and regulates the ways it carries out its life. Here we have before our eyes nothing less than the connection of cognitive and normative attitudes, manners of behavior, and processes by which human life directs itself with regard to what is beneficial to life and what is detrimental to life.

But how could this uncommonly strong and integrative activity of specifying what is beneficial to life and what is detrimental to life *not* be the "principle of the return to God's image"?


## Mere Autonomy: The Wretchedness of Sinners

We still have to examine the second important element of Gen. 3:22. We have to examine what is meant by saying: "See, the human being has become like one of us." What does this passage say for or against an equation between God and humankind? In the exclusive concentration upon the individual, the expression "knowing good and evil" could be interpreted in such a way that one could clearly see the continuing difference between humankind and God with regard to the finitude of the human individual. With regard to knowing (*jd`*), one could then point out that "the comparison is valid only with regard to the human consciousness (that is, the consciousness present in the finite individual)."[21] With regard to the *activity* of humankind in the context as a whole, one could on good exegetical grounds push the following claim: "With this capacity human beings have indeed become 'like God' . . . but not God. For what is in truth beneficial or detrimental to human beings does not devolve upon the self-determination of the human subject, but remains Yahweh's prerogative."[22]

The text, though, requires us to focus not only on an individual and the individual's behavior, but upon a powerful ordering process executed by humanity for humanity. Since the text requires that, it does indeed seem to pose the problem of distinguishing between God and humankind. In "knowing good and evil" we have before us an ordering behavior and ordering event aimed at the organization of the realm of human life with regard to what is beneficial and detrimental to that life. That ordering behavior and ordering event transcend the intellectual behavior and capacity of the individual. The continuing difference between God and humankind can no longer be determined from the perspective of the limited capacity and talent of the individual.

Does not the constellation of God and species in fact require recognition of an equation between God and humankind? At this point, in this situation the temptation is great to join the Reformers in taking flight to God's "irony."[23] The alternative is to take very seriously that Old Testament thought always comes from the perspective of unity, "from the perspective of commonality,"[24] and to see clearly that the text explicitly emphasizes Adam's *isolation*. If we take seriously that the Old Testament thinks from the perspective of unity and commonality, the *explicit emphasis upon a comparison* is already a warning signal in itself! The fact that the comparison is thematized at all announces the sharpest conceivable differentiation. It deprives human beings of the possibility of themselves determining the difference as such. The text confirms for human beings an ordering behavior that determines and encompasses human thought and life. But the differentiation mentioned above remains inaccessible to that ordering behavior. In a way of thinking that moves from the perspective of unity and commonality, "See, the human being has become like one of us" expresses the differentiation that is then tangibly carried through: the separation of human beings from God.

The dilemma of fallen humanity becomes still clearer when we observe that Gen. 3:22 emphasizes the fallen humanity's being *echad—us—*and thus being isolated in the midst of a plurality. For traditions of interpretation it has been a riddle how the content of this plurality—Adam has become like one of *us*—is to be more closely specified. The angels, the Trinity, the community of God and God's creatures, or simply the royal "we" have been weighed as candidates for specifying the *us*. With regard to our theme we can consciously leave this question open and concentrate upon the *fact of Adam's isolation*. Adam has become like one of us, like a solitary one of us—we are to read that strictly and literally. We are not to flatten it out as if what stood in the text were only *kamônû*, like us.

At the same time we are not to reduce the *echad* in an individualistic manner, if we want to do justice to the phrase "knowing good and evil." Adam is not only an individual come of age. Adam encompasses the entire species. Adam who "knows good and evil" stands for an agent and realm of power encompassing the entire species. In a whole variety of ways, this agent of power is in itself intersubjectively and consensually self-confirming, self-empowering, and self-ensuring. Yet with all that, and with his impressive knowledge of what is beneficial to life and what is detrimental to life, and with his corresponding intersubjective ordering behavior, this Adam is—relative to God and God's creation—a single solitary one, an *echad*!

Through the fall autonomous human beings have loosed themselves from the community of creation, from the association of relations of interdependence[25] grounded and intended by God. Now human beings are only autonomous, only self-determining. Now they follow only their own perspectives on what is beneficial and detrimental only to their life. At the same time human beings intersubjectively shore up and fortify themselves in their solitariness and isolation. At the same time they are able in their solitariness and isolation to perceive and to determine in their solitary and isolated way what is beneficial and detrimental to their life. Because of this, human beings fall into a situation *structured by enormous delusion.* They fancy themselves free, superior, secure, powerful, indeed equal to God. They think that they have their life fully in hand and under control. In their relative power they can overlay and deaden all sensitivity to the isolation into which they have come. They do not even notice how in mere autonomy they live in disregard of the laws and vital orders of the other areas of creaturely life. They do not even notice their infractions against those laws. They do not notice how in their relative power they destructively introduce themselves into creation, boring their way into it. They do not notice how in doing so they whitewash over and seek to repress their isolation and their being *echad.*

Perhaps it has been reserved for our own time to experience with particular ferocity this violent and dangerous self-isolation of human beings from of the rest of creation. The fact can no longer be repressed from individual and public consciousness that the societies of our day are exploiting, devastating and destroying their natural, cultural, and psychic environments with breathtaking speed and brutality. It can no longer be repressed that these processes of exploitation and destruction will have and have already had fatal repercussions. Undeniable and dangerous repercussions are already at hand, although the developments that have triggered them are, measured on a world-historical scale, still brand new.

Measured on a world-historical scale, the systematic electrification of the world, the systematic covering of the world with roads and automobiles, and the chemical transformation of agriculture are still young. Their worldwide effect is perhaps one human lifespan old. Measured on a world-historical scale, high-tech developments—developments such as nuclear technology and microelectronics—have hardly begun. Similarly, international air traffic, mass tourism, and comfortably consumable electronic mass communication have been routine for only half a human lifespan. Only the last few decades have seen the growth of garbage mountains in the industrialized nations and the spread of the mass media's fog of entertainment garbage. Despite their short existence these and other factors have already added up to violent forms of interference into the natural, cultural, and psychic foundations of our life. The infinitely broad and stable world, capable of bearing any burden, was an illusion. Are human beings who by their own powers know and enact what is beneficial and detrimental to life also proving to be an illusion?

It is the destruction of natural and cultural environments that has forever ruined for us any retreat into the anthropocentric worldview. The destruction of natural environments is manifest. The destruction of cultural environments remains less readily grasped. Both have deeply shaken our trust in the capacity of human knowledge to be controlled and meaningfully developed. We are beginning to notice the dangerously one-sided and selective characteristics of a knowledge of what is beneficial to life and what is detrimental to life when that knowledge is isolated and tuned only by and for human intersubjectivity. We are seized by the fear that selective ways of opening up reality, when they are massively pushed forward, lead first to distortions in our perception of reality and then to the destruction of the life-promoting relations of creaturely interdependence.

In reaction to this development most of the powerful societies of our day have begun to place themselves in a condition of perpetual self-alarm within important subdivisions of the society. But creaturely, sinful self-isolation of the human race also encompasses the political, mass-media, and moral communication aimed at saving us from the current condition. The great worldwide moral market, with its communications of reciprocal recognition, does not break through the self-isolation of human beings who in the context of created reality are only autonomous. The great processes that keep our moral, political, and mass-media markets in action are set in motion according to human standards of measurement of what is beneficial to life and what is detrimental to life. Attention is given and attention is promised, attention is withdrawn or its withdrawal is envisioned, all according to human standards of measurement of what is beneficial to life and what is detrimental to life.

Knowledge of the connection between creation and sin cultivates sensitivity to this collective powerlessness and self-disempowerment. It discloses the connection between the relative power and intracreaturely self-isolation of the human species.[26] It makes possible an understanding of the destructive and, at the same time, blind and helpless power in which the human species endangers and destroys its environments and consequently itself. In so doing the human species decides what is beneficial to life and what is detrimental to life from its own simultaneously powerful and extremely limited perspective. Humanity that is *only* autonomous does not have under control the conditions and laws of the realms of life into which it as a creature is bound. Knowledge of creation does not thereby offer any theological solutions, and even less any quick practical remedies. Creation is not yet atonement and redemption. Nevertheless, a realistic, biblically oriented theology of creation is indispensable in fending off false promises of solutions and in honing the eye for productive approaches to paths out of the danger. The totalizing and the reductionist conceptions of creation have proved themselves to be inadequate. The same is true of merely anthropocentric attempts at gaining access to the doctrine of creation.

By contrast, the biblical traditions understand creation as a determinate and differentiated association of creaturely realms, which both penetrates and overarches our perceptions and our schemes of reality. This association of creaturely realms is for our apparently unbiased common-sense perception overly complex, in part strange and in part inaccessible. The problematic relation between creation and reality and the dilemmas of "natural revelation" have shown this to us, as did our reflections on angelology and on the theme of creation and sin. Moreover, creation does not hang together in a way that is devoid of conflicts and devoid of inequality in power relations. The doctrine of heaven and earth and the much-controverted "mandate of dominion" document this, as do our most recent reflections on creation and sin. Yet biblically oriented theological corrections to the apparently unbiased common-sense perception of "reality" did not lead into the realms of mere speculation or pure fantasy. Instead they led to a sharpened perception: on the one hand, sharpened perception of realities and associations of realities that have been culturally repressed; on the other hand, sharpened perception of reductionist ways of perceiving that merely by long repetition have become accepted as "normal" and "going without saying."

Biblically oriented perception of creation sharpens and enriches the perception of the "realities in which we live." Precisely with regard to the dangerous connection between self-isolation and self-expression—a connection that is characteristic of human existence fallen under the power of sin—witnesses many centuries old from the biblical traditions prove themselves to be vital and illuminating even in the midst of the afflictions of our time and our world. Biblically oriented knowledge of creation cultivates sensitivity to relations of power, relations of powerlessness, and the manifold ways in which the two are interlaced both in heaven and on earth. Biblically oriented knowledge of creation heightens the experience of human distress—but it also sharpens the perception of the divine powers whose goal is the deliverance of human beings. The knowledge of creation makes us sensitive to repressed areas and conflicts in the realities in which we live and contributes to the renewal of our outworn definitions and schemes of reality.

# notes

## Introduction

1. "Creation or Emanation: Two Paradigms of Reason," in D. Burrell and B. McGinn, eds., *God and Creation: An Ecumenical Symposium* (Notre Dame, Ind.: University of Notre Dame Press, 1990), 27ff., 29. See also D. Burrell, *Knowing the Unknowable God: Ibn-Sina, Maimonides, Aquinas* (Notre Dame, Ind.: University of Notre Dame Press, 1986).

2. Burrell, *Knowing the Unknowable God,* 2; cf. 3 and passim (emphasis mine).

3. "Grundprobleme der Gotteslehre," in E. Herms, *Offenbarung und Glaube: Zur Bildung des christlichen Lebens* (Tübingen: Mohr, 1992), 343ff. See "Afterword."

4. Ibid., 348–49.

5. From the 1802 journal as cited by W. Dilthey, *Leben Schleiermachers,* vol. 1, *Gesammelte Schriften* 13 (Göttingen: Vandenhoeck: 1970), 323.

6. With regard to the great difficulties and the still greater opportunities of this collaboration, see P. D. Miller, "Can Two Walk Together without an Appointment?" *Theology Today* 52 (1995): 169ff.

## Chapter 1. What Is Creation? Rereading Genesis 1 and 2

1. This chapter is a revised version of "What Is 'Creation?' Rereading Genesis 1 and 2," *Theology Today* 48 (1991): 56–71.

2. "The Biblical Understanding of Creation in the Bible and in Jewish Tradition," in *Ex Auditu,* vol. 3, *Creation,* ed. T. Gillespie (1987): 98ff., 106; cf. also 99.

3. K. Barth, *Church Dogmatics* 3/1, ed. G. W. Bromiley and T. F. Torrance, trans. J. W. Edwards et al. (Edinburgh: T. and T. Clark, 1958), 94ff.

4. Here I am thinking primarily of Phyllis Trible, *God and the Rhetoric of Sexuality* (Philadelphia: Fortress, 1978), and of the discussion touched off by her book.

5. See also the efforts of Gershom Scholem and Jürgen Moltmann to take up Isaak Luria's doctrine of *zimzum* so as to give theological determinacy to "nothing" (J. Moltmann, *God in Creation: A New Theology of Creation and the Spirit of God*, trans. M. Kohl [Minneapolis: Fortress, 1993], 86ff.). With regard to this noteworthy new direction, cf. Eberhard Jüngel, "Gottes ursprüngliches Anfangen als schöpferische Selbstbegrenzung: Ein Beitrag zum Gespräch mit Hans Jonas über den 'Gottesbegriff nach Auschwitz,'" in H. Deuser et al., eds., *Gottes Zukunft—Zukunft der Welt: Festschrift für Jürgen Moltmann zum 60. Geburtstag* (Munich: Chr. Kaiser, 1986), 265ff., esp. 271ff.

6. V. Harvey, *A Handbook of Theological Terms* (New York and London: 1964), 62. In a similar vein, *The Westminster Dictionary of Christian Theology* (Philadelphia: Westminster, 1983) states that the doctrine of creation asserts that God's relationship with the world "is one of dependence and that every existing thing depends upon God for its existence, whereas God depends upon nothing outside himself" (129).

7. For Ratzinger's critique of the use of the concept of causality and his definition of creation with expressions such as "posit" and "originate," see J. Ratzinger, "Schöpfung," *Lexikon für Theologie und Kirche* vol. 9, 460ff., esp. 460–61. Gloege begins—along with a similar warning—in a more differentiated way: "The concept [creation] comprehensively governs the statements about the relation of the triune God to humankind and the world. In terms of content, creation is directed toward Israel's election and toward the reconciliation of the world accomplished in Jesus Christ." But in developing this, Gloege gives fundamental place to the abstract definitions of God's "strict *transcendence*" "over against the world" and to the "*free positing of the beginning*" (G. Gloege, "Schöpfung: Dogmatics," in *Die Religion in Geschichte und Gegenwart*, 3d ed., vol. 5, 1484ff., 1484 and 1485–86. The section on the history of religions identifies "consciousness of creation" with "religious consciousness of causality" (C.-M. Edsman, ibid., 1469). This abstraction also makes its mark on exegetical investigations that are otherwise quite subtle and nonsimplistic. For example K. Eberlein writes that "as a word of our language, 'creation'—to the extent that it is used in a religious framework . . . circumscribes both the beginning of reality and present reality itself" (K. Eberlein, *Gott der Schöpfer—Israels Gott: Eine exegetisch-hermeneutische Studie zur theologischen Funktion alttestamentlicher Schöpfungsaussagen*, Beiträge zur Erforschung des Alten Testaments und des antiken Judentums, vol. 5 [Frankfurt: 1986], 93ff., 99). In the effort to defend against other faulty abstractions, Eberlein—following so to speak the principle of "the lesser of two evils"—maintains that this linguistic arrangement is thoroughly supported exegetically (ibid., 99–100).

8. Kenneth Cauthen, *Systematic Theology: A Modern Protestant Approach* (Lewiston and Queenston: 1986), 131. See also Nahum M. Sarna,

*Understanding Genesis: The Heritage of Biblical Israel* (New York: Schocken Books, 1970), 3: The account "tells us something about the nature of the one God who is the Creator and supreme sovereign of the world and whose will is absolute. It asserts that God is outside the realm of nature, which is wholly subservient to Him."

9. Ferdinand Christian Baur, *Lehrbuch der christlichen Dogmengeschichte,* vol. 3 (Leipzig: 1867), 370–71.

10. Leo Scheffczyk, *Einführung in die Schöpfungslehre* (Darmstadt: 1982), 5.

11. For an insightful treatment, see L. Schmidt, "Schöpfung: Natur und Geschichte," in H. J. Boecker et al., *Neukirchener Arbeitsbücher: Altes Testament* (Neukirchen-Vluyn: Neukirchener, 1983), 243ff.

12. See Trible, *God and the Rhetoric of Sexuality,* 73ff.

13. Biblical quotations are based on the New Revised Standard Version, with adaptations to comport with the wording of the original German text— *Trans.*

14. L. White, "The Historical Roots of Our Ecological Crisis," in *Science* 155 (1967). On this point Odil Hannes Steck is particularly instructive, along with summarizing the more recent discussion (O. H. Steck, "Dominium Terrae: Zum Verhältnis von Mensch und Schöpfung in Genesis 1," in F. Stolz, ed., *Religiöse Wahrnehmung der Welt* [Zürich: Theologischer Verlag Zürich, 1988], 89–105, esp. 89.)

15. Chap. 5 of this book treats the relation between creation and the mandate of dominion. Picking up on recent Jewish and Christian exegetical discussion, I have tried elsewhere to make some progress in the difficult work of illuminating the connection between creation and cultic life. See M. Welker, "Creation: Big Bang or the Work of Seven Days?" *Theology Today* 52 (1995): 173–87.

16. Cf. chap. 3 of this book. It is disputed whether Gen. 1:20 emphasizes aquatic life's own reproductive activity (cf. Ex. 7:28). See O. H. Steck, *Der Schöpfungsbericht der Priesterschrift: Studien zur literarkritischen und über- lieferungsgeschichtlichen Problematik von Genesis 1,1–2,4a,* 2d ed., Forschungen zur Religion und Literatur des alten und neuen Testaments 115 (Göttingen: Vandenhoeck, 1981), 62, n. 222.

17. For a rejection of the attempt to understand Genesis 1 as the fusion of two creation accounts—an attempt that is also popular with regard to the quandary under discussion here—see Steck, *Schöpfungsbericht,* esp. 11ff.

18. On this point O. H. Steck is very instructive ("Der Wein unter den Schöpfungsgaaben: Überlegungen zu Psalm 104," in *Wahrnehmungen Gottes im Alten Testament: Gesammelte Studien,* Theologische Bücherei [Munich: Kaiser, 1982], 240ff.).

19. "Relations of interdependence" are not to be understood as an arbitrary, always contingent connectedness of living beings and realms of life that could just as well exist independently of each other. I. U. Dalferth seems to have read my reflections in this way (*Der auferweckte Gekreuzigte: Zur Grammatik der Christologie* [Tübingen: Mohr, 1994], 58–59). He equates relations of interdependence with contexts of interaction. As much as I agree with him that God's creation is to be understood as "creation out of nonbeing" or mediation "through nonbeing" (ibid.), I must insist that in that regard we must engage not merely in metaphysical reflection (however this might be possible) on "nothingness," but also in reflection on the nonbeing of specific creatures and specific creatureliness. It is precisely this that is made possible by the conception of relations of interdependence, if they are not confused with mere contexts of interaction. For Dalferth the general difference between "nothingness" and "something" is important. By comparison, I think that the specific nonbeing of creatures outside of "associations of interdependent relations" needs to have theological light cast upon it. I see the decisive difference between our positions in the fact that Dalferth ultimately tries to retain the theism of abstract omnipotence and ubiquity: "Wherever God acts, something new comes out of nothing. And God acts whenever and wherever something is, at every time and in every place in the world" (ibid., 59). In my opinion these are religious or popular-philosophical opinions that, while they have certainly made a great impact in the history of Western culture, are supported neither by the biblical traditions nor by human experiences and knowledge of the world. By no means is God actively and creatively present in every point of space-time. If the biblical texts wanted to develop this type of abstract concept of ubiquity and omnipresence, they would not be able to speak, for instance, of God's Spirit withdrawing; of God's face being turned away, lowered, and veiled; of the Spirit being extinguished, being driven away, or fleeing. Nor can every banal or destructive "something . . . at every time and in every place in the world" be attributed to God's creative action. Of course, Dalferth's concept can appear compatible with the thesis that "nothing is simpler than God" (I. U. Dalferth, *Gott: Philosophisch-theologische Denkversuche* [Tübingen: Mohr, 1992], 1).

20. The expression "creaturely realms" needs to be developed in greater detail. For the moment let me merely refer to that state of affairs on which Gen. 1 focuses with the frequent repetition of the expression "according to its kind." See also the reflections on the differentiation of heaven and earth in chap. 3 of this volume.

21. Cf. M. Welker, *Universalität Gottes und Relativität der Welt: Theologische Kosmologie im Dialog mit dem amerikanischen Prozeßdenken nach Whitehead*, rev. ed. (Neukirchen-Vluyn: Neukirchener, 1988), esp. 32ff.,

203ff. These ideas are picked up by Moltmann, *God in Creation*, 158ff. See also M. Welker, "Himmel," *Evangelisches Kirchenlexikon*, 3d ed. (1988), 519ff.

22. Cf. O. Keel, *Die Welt der altorientalischen Bildsymbolik und das Alte Testament: Am Beispiel der Psalmen*, 4th ed. (Neukirchen: Neukirchener, 1984), as well as chap. 4 of the present book.

23. See Welker, "Creation: Big Bang or the Work of Seven Days?" 131ff.

24. Cf. chap. 3 below.

25. Patrick D. Miller has illuminated in various perspectives the *plurality* of the "divine world" and its dynamics. I refer the reader, for example, to the following two works of his: *Genesis 1–11: Studies in Structure and Theme*, J.S.O.T., Supplement Series 8 (Sheffield: 1978), esp. 9ff.; "Cosmology and World Order in the Old Testament: The Divine Council as Cosmic-Political Symbol," in *Horizons in Biblical Theology: An International Dialogue* 9 (1987): 53ff. I expect that there will be a lot to learn—also in the systematic realm—from the contemporary discussion of the connections between temple and creation and between temple and heaven. See the contribution made by B. Janowski in "Tempel und Schöpfung: Schöpfungstheologische Aspekte der priesterschriftlichen Heiligtumskonzeption," in *Schöpfung und Neuschöpfung, Jahrbuch für biblische Theologie* 5 (Neukirchen-Vluyn: Neukirchener, 1990). Janowski's article is developed in continuous dialogue especially with P. Weimar, "Sinai und Schöpfung: Komposition und Theologie der priesterschriftlichen Sinaigeschichte," *Revue Biblique* 95 (1988): 337–85; and E. Zenger, *Gottes Bogen in den Wolken: Untersuchungen zu Komposition und Theologie der priesterschriftlichen Urgeschichte*, Stuttgarter Bibelstudien 112, 2d ed. (Stuttgart: Katholisches Bibelwerk, 1987).

26. See C. Kloos, *YHWH's Combat with the Sea* (Leiden: 1986); and J. Day, *God's Conflict with the Dragon and the Sea: Echoes of a Canaanite Myth in the Old Testament*, 2d ed. (Cambridge: Cambridge University Press, 1988).

27. Here I would like to make only two very general references: first, to the recent international discussion of the connection between creation theology and reign-of-God theology (see B. Janowski, "Das Königtum Gottes in den Psalmen: Bemerkungen zu einem neuen Gesamtentwurf," *Zeitschrift für Theologie und Kirche* 86 [1989]: 389ff.; as well as J. Jeremias, *Das Königtum Gottes in den Psalmen*, Forschungen zur Religion und Literatur des Alten und Neuen Testaments 141 [Göttingen: 1987]); second, to new theological, cosmological and epistemological perspectives proposed by H.-P. Müller (e.g., "Eine neue babylonische Menschenschöpfungserzählung im Licht keilschriftlicher und biblischer Parallelen: Zur Wirklichkeitsauffassung im Mythos," *Orientalia* 58/1 [1989]: 61ff., esp. 80ff.; "Segen im Alten Testament: Theologische Implikationen eines halb vergessenen Themas," *Zeitschrift für Theologie und Kirche* 87 [1990]: 1ff., esp. 20ff.).

28. From among the large body of literature that has been appearing on this topic, see J. Moltmann's theology of creation and B. W. Anderson, "Creation and Ecology," in *Creation in the Old Testament* (Philadelphia: Fortress Press, 1984), 152ff.; U. Duchrow and G. Liedke, *Schalom: Der Schöpfung Befreiung, den Menschen Gerechtigkeit, den Völkern Frieden* (Stuttgart: Kohlhammer, 1987); G. Rau et al., *Frieden in der Schöpfung: Das Naturverständnis protestantischer Theologie* (Gütersloh: Gütersloher, 1987); Committee on Social Witness Policy, Presbyterian Church (U.S.A.), *Keeping and Healing the Creation* (Louisville: 1989).

29. A closer investigation of these interdependencies would need to elaborate the concept of creation more precisely. After all, it is by no means the case that every cultural construction or every cultural intervention is "creative." See the articles on the themes: "Nature as Object of the Natural Sciences," "Nature as Raw Material," "Nature as Landscape and Garden," "Nature as Aesthetic Event," and "Nature as Social and Technical Construction," in Landeshauptstadt Stuttgart, Kulturamt, ed., *Zum Naturbegriff der Gegenwart*, 2 vol. (Stuttgart: Frommann, 1994).

30. The differentiations of the concept of nature within the spectrum of recent contributions to the theology of creation are elucidated by E. M. Hartlieb, "Natur als Schöpfung: Zum Begriff der Natur in der jüngsten protestantischen Theologie" (Ph.D. diss., Ruprecht-Karls-Universität Heidelberg, 1993).

31. I am grateful to the physicist and theologian Christoph Wassermann for pointing out to me in personal correspondence that both relativity theory and quantum theory are based in theoretical models in which absolute and relative totalizations, monistic and pluralistic thought, are bound together. "In the special theory of relativity this is true for the connection of an infinite multitude of possible relative systems of reference with the nature and description of the electromagnetic field that is common to all of them in the same way. An example from quantum theory is the new monistic and abstract description of the physical reality that in experimental investigations is concretized in a pluralistic way (as a group of particles or as a complex field)."

32. A. N. Whitehead, *Science and the Modern World* (New York: Macmillan, 1947), 85–86.

33. See ibid., 86; cf. 126–27.

34. Ibid., 86. See also 96–97; and A. N. Whitehead, *Process and Reality: An Essay in Cosmology*, corrected edition, ed. D. R. Griffin and D. W. Sherburne (New York: Free Press, 1979), 10, 14ff. and passim.

35. Whitehead, *Science and the Modern World*, 86.

36. "Although that majestic chapter could have lost its credibility through the endless series of interpretations given to it as age followed age, it has

retained a unique appeal through the ages in proof of its intrinsic soundness" (S. L. Jaki, *Genesis 1 through the Ages* [London: Thomas More, 1992], 301).

37. See chap. 5 and 6, below, as well as Welker, "Creation: Big Bang or the Work of Seven Days?"

## Chapter 2. Creation and the Problem of Natural Revelation

1. J. Calvin, *Institutes of the Christian Religion*, trans. H. Beveridge, vol. 1 (Grand Rapids, Mich.: Eerdmans, 1957).

2. *Institutes* I,3,1.

3. Ibid., I,3,1; I,3,3.

4. Ibid., I,3,3.

5. Cf. Lev. 26:36.

6. *Institutes* I,3,2.

7. Ibid., I,3,2, trans. altered.

8. See D. Henrich, "Die Grundstruktur der modernen Philosophie," in H. Ebeling, *Subjektivität und Selbsterhaltung: Beiträge zur Diagnose der Moderne* (Frankfurt: Suhrkamp, 1976), 97ff.

9. Cf. the controversy documented by C. Bresch et al., eds., *Kann man Gott aus der Natur erkennen? Evolution als Offenbarung* (Freiburg: Herder, 1990). This volume is unable to provide a clear answer.

10. *Institutes* I,4,3.

11. Ibid., I,3,1; trans. altered.

12. Cf. M. Welker, "Auf der theologischen Suche nach einem 'Weltethos' in einer Zeit kurzlebiger moralischer Märkte: Küng, Tracy und die Bedeutung der neuen Biblischen Theologie," *Evangelische Theologie* 55/5 (1995), 438–56.

13. *Institutes* I,3,3.

14. Ibid., I,5,14.

15. Ibid., I,5,15.

16. See chap. 6 of this volume.

17. Cf. R. Bultmann, "Der Begriff der Offenbarung im Neuen Testament," in *Glauben und Verstehen*, vol. 3 (Tübingen: Mohr, 1965), 1ff.

18. One can join E. Herms ("Offenbarung und Wahrheit," in *Offenbarung und Glaube*, 273ff.) in speaking of a "process of manifestation," if it is made clear that the christological and pneumatological dimensions of revelation are necessary for the manifestation of the "ground and object of Christian faith" (cf. 275). Even the combination of creation and revelation remains deficient in this regard.

## Chapter 3. Creation as the Heavens and the Earth

1. K. Barth, *The Epistle to the Romans*, trans. E. C. Hoskyns (London: Oxford University Press, 1933), 10.

2. With regard to the differentiation and correlation of the aspects (1) "cosmos as herald of the power and majesty" of God and (2) "heaven as the domain and dwelling" of God, see C. Houtman, *Der Himmel im Alten Testament: Israels Weltbild und Weltanschauung* (Leiden: Brill, 1993), esp. 139ff., 319ff.

3. L. Feuerbach, *The Essence of Christianity*, trans. G. Eliot (New York: Harper and Row, 1957), 170ff., 175.

4. Ibid., 172.

5. Ibid., 173.

6. Cf. chapter 1 of this volume.

7. Cf. K. Barth, "Der Christ in der Gesellschaft," in J. Moltmann, ed., *Anfänge der dialektischen Theologie*, 5th ed., Theologische Bücherei 17:1 (Munich: Kaiser, 1985), 9, 12, 13, 21, and *passim*.

8. Barth, "Der Christ in der Gesellschaft," 34.

9. A. C. Cochrane, ed., *Reformed Confessions of the Sixteenth Century* (Philadelphia: Westminster, 1966), 329.

10. Ezra, Nehemiah, Judith, and Daniel.

11. Cf. Macc. 3:19, 60; 4:10 and passim.

12. Alfred North Whitehead, *Science and the Modern World* (New York: Macmillan, 1947), 263.

13. See also the following chapter.

14. For a more detailed treatment, see Michael Welker, "Creation: Big Bang or the Work of Seven Days?" *Theology Today* 52 (1995): 173–87.

15. Barth, *Church Dogmatics*, 3/1, ed. G. W. Bromiley and T. F. Torrance, trans. J. W. Edwards et al. (Edinburgh: T. and T. Clark, 1958), 143.

16. Cf. chap. 1 of this book.

17. Barth, *CD* 3/1, 153.

18. One also encounters this way of thinking in the New Testament traditions. See K. Berger, *Manna, Mehl und Sauerteig: Korn und Brot im Alltag der frühen Christen* (Stuttgart: Quell, 1993), 28ff.; G. Theissen, "Der Bauer und die von selbst Frucht bringende Erde: Naiver Synergismus in Mk 4,26–29," *Zeitschrift für die Neutestamentliche Wissenschaft und die Kund der älteren Kirche* 85 (1994): 167ff. With regard to the systematic-theological search for a materially and theological appropriate conceptuality, cf. J. Lovelock, *The Ages of Gaia: A Biography of Our Living Earth* (New York: 1988); R. Ruether, *Gaia and God: An Ecofeminist Theology of Earth Healing*

(London: SCM, 1993); and the issue *Gott und Gaja: Zur Theologie der Erde, Evangelische Theologie* 53 (1993).

19. Steck, *Schöpfungsbericht der Priesterschrift: Studien zur literarkritischen und überlieferungsgeschichtlichen Problematik von Genesis 1, 1–2, 4a,* 2d ed., Forschungen zur Religion und Literatur des alten und neuen Testaments 115 (Göttingen: Vandenhoeck, 1981), 93–94.

20. Ibid., 121–22.

21. Ibid., 129.

## Chapter 4. Angels and God's Presence in Creation

1. F. Schleiermacher, *The Christian Faith,* ed. H. R. Mackintosh and J. S. Stewart (New York: Harper and Row, 1963), 159, 160.

2. In this chapter I am taking up ideas from C. Westermann, *God's Angels Need No Wings,* trans. D. L. Scheidt (Philadelphia: Fortress, 1979).

3. I owe to an unpublished lecture by Hartmut Gese on "Angels in the Old Testament" the important idea that in specific layers of the Old Testament we need to reckon with an identity between God and God's angel. Gese warns against simply assuming the angels' inferiority to Yahweh. This recognition was important in spurring me to pose this question. Cf. G. MacGregor, *Angels: Ministers of Grace* (New York: Paragon House, 1988), 25.

4. G. von Rad sensed this problem but conceived it as a problem (and ultimately a transcendental-theoretical one) of human perception: "When God enters the apperception of man, the angel of God is introduced" See G. Kittel, ed., *Theological Dictionary of the New Testament,* vol. 1, trans. and ed. G.W. Bromiley (Grand Rapids, Mich.: Eerdmans, 1964), 77.

5. My wife and I once heard in Chicago a performance of Mahler's Seventh Symphony, directed by Claudio Abbado, that we were convinced differed from all our earlier experiences of concerts in such a clear and striking way, that I can readily imagine that people of other times and cultures were able to differentiate specific unique encounters with beings of a human sort in such a clear way from other encounters that they took themselves to be experiencing another "reality." In saying this I do not wish to offer a psychologizing "explanation" of angelic appearances. Nor do I wish to claim that these days angelology has its equivalent in exceptional experiences of music, even when these are often celebrated by the secular culture of our day as religious forms and contents.

6. Westermann, *God's Angels,* 12.

7. Ibid., 58 (cf. 70, 75, 104–105, 124).

8. See the blessing pronounced by Jacob as he is dying in Gen. 48:15-16:

"The *God* before whom my ancestors Abraham and Isaac walked, the *God* who has been my shepherd all my life to this day, the *angel* who has redeemed me from all harm. . . ."

9. Cf. W. Gross, *Bileam: Literar- und formkritische Untersuchungen der Prosa in Num 22–24*, Studien zum Alten und Neuen Testament (Munich: Kösel, 1974), 355ff.

10. Westermann, *God's Angels*, 45.

11. Ibid.

12. Cf. G. von Rad's sermon on Joshua 5:13-15 in his *Predigten*, ed. U. von Rad (Munich: Kaiser, 1972), 154ff.

13. Westermann, *God's Angels*, 63–64.

14. Ibid., 61, trans. altered.

15. Ibid., 58, 109.

16. Unfortunately, the complex of themes associated with the word "angels" is one of those areas in which not only does imaginative individual sensibility let the powers of fantasy roam hither and yon, but publishers and authors especially like to transform the great religious traditions into entertaining material to be manipulated at will. Angels are particularly vulnerable to the pollution and destruction of the cultural environment. They are indeed "an endangered species" (M. Godwin, *Angels—An Endangered Species* (Bellevue, Wash.: S. and S. Kenmore, 1990).

17. With regard to the rare and late fusion of the two angelologies, see V. Hirth, *Gottes Boten im Alten Testament: Die alttestamentliche Mal'ak-Vorstellung unter besonderer Berücksichtigung des Mal'ak-Jahwe-Problems*, Theologische Arbeiten (Berlin: 1976), 108–109.

18. Regarding the "they," cf. M. Heidegger, *Being and Time*, trans. J. Macquarrie and E. Robinson (New York: Harper and Row, 1962), esp. §27.

19. Cf. especially the instances of the use of *mal'ak* in Judges 1 and 2 Samuel 25, as well as in 1 and 2 Kings.

20. Cf. D. Bonhoeffer, *The Communion of the Saints: A Dogmatic Inquiry into the Sociology of the Church*, trans. R. G. Smith et al. (New York: Harper and Row, 1963), 50–51, 67ff., 82ff.

21. Karl Barth in his angelology does not see this clearly enough. See his *Church Dogmatics* 3/3, ed. G. W. Bromiley and T. F. Torrance, trans. J. W. Edwards et al. (Edinburgh: T. and T. Clark, 1958). A differentiated correlation between angels as messengers and angels as members of the heavenly assembly of those who are glorifying God could have induced Barth to confront a fundamental problem of the *Church Dogmatics*: the unclear specification of the relation between God's sovereignty (*Herrschaft*) and God's glory (*Herrlichkeit*).

22. Westermann, *God's Angels*, 24, 25.

23. Ibid., 23. U. Wolff, *Breit aus die Flügel beide: Von den Engeln des Lebens* (Freiburg: Herder, 1993) provides a regrettable example of the use of angelology for its entertainment value, with the result that angelology's substantive intentions and rationalities are misunderstood and distorted, and ultimately both God and human beings receive wings. See M. Welker, "Kraut und Rüben über Engel," *Lutherische Monatschriften* 12 (1993): 42–43.

24. Cf. also chap. 3.

25. In the recent past E. Peterson reflected upon this in "Von den Engeln," in his *Theologische Traktate* (Munich: Kösel, 1951), 323ff., esp. 327ff. Cf. also K. Berger, "Volksversammlung und Gemeinde Gottes: Zu den Anfängen der christologischen Verwendung von 'Ekklesia,'" *Zeitschrift für Theologie und Kirche* 73 (1976): 167ff., esp. 194ff.; O. Hofius, "Gemeinschaft mit den Engeln im Gottesdienst der Kirche: Eine traditionsgeschichtliche Skizze," *Zeitschrift für Theologie und Kirche* 89 (1992): 172ff.

26. Westermann, *God's Angels*, 35ff., 75–76, 92–93, 102–103, and passim.

27. J. Moltmann, *The Crucified God: The Cross of Christ as the Foundation and Criticism of Christian Theology*, trans. R.A. Wilson and J. Bowden (New York: Harper and Row, 1974), 329–32.

28. Cf. H. Schlier, "Die Engel nach dem Neuen Testament," in *Besinnung auf das Neue Testament: Exegetische Aufsätze und Vorträge*, vol. 2, 2d ed. (Freiburg: Herder, 1967), esp. 161ff.

29. Cf. esp. 1 Thess. 3:13; Mark 8:38; Matt. 13:41; 16:27; 24:31; 25:31; Luke 9:26; 2 Thess. 1:7. Concerning the connection between the theology of the Human One and the "scenery around the throne of God," cf. K. Berger, *Theologiegeschichte des Urchristentums: Theologie des Neuen Testaments* (Tübingen: Francke, 1994), 297ff.

30. First steps are offered by J. Daniélou, *The Angels and Their Mission according to the Fathers of the Church*, trans. D. Heimann (Westminster, Md.: Christian Classics, 1987); M. Seeman, "Die Engel," in *Mysterium Salutis*, vol. 2, ed. J. Feiner and M. Löhrer, 3d ed. (Einsiedeln: Benziger, 1978), esp. 968ff.

31. "Power is not foreign to angels, but is an essential manner of their being" (Schlier, *Die Engel*, 164). Cf. L. Scheffczyk, *Einführung in die Schöpfungslehre*, 2d ed. (Darmstadt: Wissenschaftliche Buchgesellschaft, 1975), 109–10, 114.

32. Cf. M. Plathow's observations on Luther's sermons on angels: "Even in the eschatological orientation on the vision of the glory of the triune God and of the perfect joy in the communion of the angels, M. Luther remains focused on the 'here' of the life of the faithful and of the church of Jesus Christ, who still stand in Christ's battle against the power of sin, the devil and death"

(M. Plathow, "Die Engel—Ein systematisch-theologisches Thema," in *Ich will mit dir sein: Kreuzestheologische Vorsehungslehre* [Berlin: Köster, 1995], 33ff., 46).

33. Concerning the eschatological public sphere, cf. M. Welker, "Hoffnung und Hoffen auf Gott," in H. Deuser et al., eds., *Gottes Zukunft— Zukunft der Welt: Festschrift für Jürgen Moltmann zum 60. Geburtstag* (Munich: Kaiser, 1986), 34ff.

34. With regard to the concept of "Christos Angelos" in the early church's interpretation of the divine appearances in the Old Testament, cf. J. Barbel, *Christos Angelos: Die Anschauung von Christus als Bote und Engel in der gelehrten und volkstümlichen Literatur des christlichen Altertums* (Bottrop: 1941). For a summary, cf. Barbel, "Christos Angelos: Die frühchristliche und patristische Engelchristologie im Lichte der neueren Forschung," in T. Bogler, ed., *Die Engel in der Welt von heute: Gesammelte Aufsätze* (Maria Laach: 1960), 89ff.

35. Cf. the first section of this chapter. Cf. also M. Welker, *Universalität Gottes und Relativität der Welt: Theologische Kosmologie im Dialog mit dem amerikanischen Prozeßdenken nach Whitehead*, 2d ed. (Neukirchen-Vluyn: Neukirchener, 1988), esp. 32ff., 203ff.; J. Moltmann, *God in Creation: A New Theology of Creation and the Spirit of God*, trans. M. Kohl (New York: Harper and Row, 1985), 158–64.

36. Certainly we can say that, according to biblical traditions, angels provide accompaniment in the transition from this earth to "another reality," to a "more developed reality." This way of speaking would be theologically defensible, but would remain very vague, since it would more closely define neither "that reality" nor the "transition" nor the particular presence or copresence of the angels. We could go on and attempt to attain more specific insights with the help of a differentiation between time, eternity, and an "eonic" existence characteristic of the angels (cf. D. Staniloae, *Orthodoxe Dogmatik*, Ökumenische Theologie 12 [Zürich: Benziger, 1985], 379ff.). Yet the constitution of our theories of time does not encourage us to consider the chances very good that this approach will provide clarification. The tedious, step-by-step process of acquiring insight into the contents of the biblical traditions and their systematic interconnections remains more promising than all abstract approaches that take two worlds or two realities as their point of departure.

37. O. Böcher calls attention to this in the article on "Angels," pt. 4, *Theologische Realenzykoläedie* 9 (1982). See his reference (598) to prototrinitarian expressions in the New Testament that arrange the angels together with Jesus Christ and the first person of the Godhead to from "a triad." Cf. Barbel, *Christos Angelos*, 105ff.; G. Stroumsa, "Le couple de l'ange et de l'esprit: Traditions juives et chrétiennes," *Revue biblique* 88 (1981): 42ff.

# Chapter 5. Creation, the Image of God, and the Mandate of Dominion

1. In our thematic context alone, see 1 Cor. 15:45, 46; Col. 3:10; Mark 10:6; Matt. 19:4; James 3:9.

2. R. Descartes, *Discours de la méthode*, intro. and notes E. Gilson, Librairie Philosophique (Paris: J. Vrin, 1979), 128; Eng.: *"Discourse on Method" and "Meditations on First Philosophy,"* trans. D. A. Cress (Indianapolis, Ind.: Hackett, 1980), 33.

3. C. Westermann, *Genesis 1–11: A Commentary*, trans. J. Scullion (Minneapolis: Augsburg, 1984), 161; cf. 147ff., 158–59. G. von Rad observes with a genteel turn of phrase that "the expressions for the exercise of this dominion are remarkably strong" (G. von Rad, *Genesis: A Commentary*, trans. J. H. Marks, Old Testament Library [Philadelphia: Westminster, 1961], 58). Westermann (158) points to parallel passages that appeal to the "Ancient Near Eastern royal ideology" in describing the violent rule of kings: 1 Kings 5:4; Ps. 110:2; 72:8; Isa. 14:6; Ezek. 34:4. Westermann also refers (161) to Jer. 34:11, 16; Neh. 5:5; 2 Chron. 28:10 (slaves); and Num. 32:22, 29; Josh. 18:1; 1 Chron. 22:18 (foreign peoples). The third section will examine these findings in light of the following investigations and with regard to recent exegetical discussion.

4. Compare already in Gen. 2:5 the observation that at first there were none of the plants of the field on earth, and no herb of the earth had yet sprung up, because: (a) Yahweh God had not caused rain to fall upon the earth, and (b) there were not yet any human beings to till the ground.

5. Cf. H. von Keler, *Theologische Beiträge* 17 (1986): 169ff.; P. Schmitz *Theologisches Jahrbuch*, Leipzig (1985): 67ff.

6. Concerning the discussion of androcentrism in Genesis 2, see the outstanding essay by P. Trible, *God and the Rhetoric of Sexuality*, Overtures to Biblical Theology 2 (Philadelphia: Fortress, 1978), 72–143.

7. Karl Barth, *Church Dogmatics* 3/1, ed. G. W. Bromiley and T. F. Torrance, trans. J. W. Edwards et al. (Edinburgh: T. and T. Clark, 1958).

8. Ibid., 207.

9. Ibid.

10. Ibid., 186.

11. Ibid.

12. Ibid., 187.

13. Ibid.

14. Cf. Barth, *CD* 3/1, esp. 288ff. See J. C. Janowski's perspicacious article, "Zur paradigmatischen Bedeutung der Geschlecterdifferenz in K. Barths

'Kirchlicher Dogmatik,'" in H. Kuhlmann, *Und drinnen waltet die züchtige Hausfrau: Zur Ethik der Geschlechterdifferenz* (Gütersloh: Kaiser, 1995), 140ff.

15. J. Moltmann, *God in Creation: A New Theology of Creation and the Spirit of God*, trans. M. Kohl (San Francisco: Harper and Row, 1985), 215ff.

16. Cf. ibid., esp. 222ff.

17. Ibid., 223.

18. Ibid.

19. See J. Moltmann, *The Trinity and the Kingdom of God: The Doctrine of God*, trans. M. Kohl (San Francisco: Harper and Row, 1981), esp. 19, 148–50; J. Moltmann, "The Inviting Unity of the Triune God," in *History and the Triune God: Contributions to Trinitarian Theology*, trans. J. Bowden (New York: Crossroad, 1992), 80ff.

20. Cf. Moltmann, *God in Creation*, 224.

21. Ibid., 217–18.

22. Ibid., 222; trans. altered.

23. Ibid.

24. Ibid., 224.

25. P. Bird, "'Male and Female He Created Them': Gen 1,27b in the Context of the Priestly Account of Creation," *Harvard Theological Review* 74 (1981): 129ff., 155.

26. Ibid., 159.

27. Ibid., 155.

28. K. Koch, "Gestaltet die Erde, doch heget das Leben! Einige Klarstellungen zum *dominium terrae* in Gen 1," in H.-G. Geyer et al., eds., *"Wenn nicht jetzt, wann dann?" Aufsätze für Hans-Joachim Kraus zum 65. Geburtstag* (Neukirchen-Vluyn: Neukirchener, 1983), 23ff.

29. N. Lohfink, "Macht euch die Erde untertan," *Orientierung* 38 (1974): 137ff.

30. Koch, "Gestaltet die Erde," 33.

31. G. Liedke has noted that the *dominium* "regulates . . . whatever material for conflict remains" See *Im Bauch des Fisches: Ökologische Theologie* (Stuttgart: Kreuz, 1979), 132.

32. A horrifying exception is discussed by J. Barr, *Biblical Faith and Natural Theology*, the Gifford Lectures for 1991 (Oxford: Clarendon, 1993), esp. 208ff.

33. C. Link, *Schöpfung: Schöpfungstheologie angesichts der Herausforderungen des 20. Jahrhunderts*, Handbuch Systematischer Theologie 7/2 (Gütersloh: Mohn, 1991), 396. Link is here picking up on Liedke, *Im Bauch des Fisches*, 130ff.

34. Concerning the indispensable connection between justice and mercy

in establishing "righteousness," see M. Welker, "Security of Expectations: Reformulating the Theology of Law and Gospel," *Journal of Religion* 66 (1986): 237ff.; M. Welker, "Gesetz und Geist," in O. Hofius and P. Stuhlmacher, eds., *Jahrbuch für biblische Theologie* 4 (Neukirchen-Vluyn: Neukirchener, 1989), 215ff.

35. E. Zenger, *Gottes Bogen in den Wolken: Untersuchungen zu Komposition und Theologie der priesterschriftlichen Urgeschichte*, 2d ed., Stuttgarter Bibelstudien 112 (Stuttgart: Katholisches Bibelwerk, 1987), 90.

36. B. Janowski, "Herrschaft über die Tiere: Gen. 1,26-28 und die Semantik von RDH," in G. Braulik, ed., *Gesellschaftlicher Wandel und biblische Theologie: Festschrift für Norbert Lohfink* (Freiburg: Herder, 1993), 183ff.

37. O. H. Steck, *World and Environment*, Biblical Encounters Series (Nashville, Tenn.: Abingdon, 1980), 106.

38. Koch, "Gestaltet die Erde," 33. Recently the extent of publications in theology and philosophy concerning justice and morality with regard to animals has been expanding remarkably. In philosophy see U. Wolf, *Das Tier in der Moral* (Frankfurt am Main: Klostermann, 1990); and the review of seven more titles by J.-C. Wolf, "Neuerscheinungen zur Tierethik," *Philosophische Rundschau* 40 (1993): 129ff. In theology cf. A. Linzey, *Christianity and the Rights of Animals* (New York: Crossroad, 1991); Kirchenamt der EKD, ed., *Zur Verantwortung des Menschen für das Tier als Mitgeschöpf: Ein Diskussionsbeitrag des Wissenschaftlichen Beirats des Beauftragten für Umweltfragen der Evangelischen Kirche in Deutschland*, EKD-Texte 41. On the latter, see E. Gräßer, *Evangelische Kommentare* 25 (1992): 7–8. For a treatment not limited to a single discipline, see E. Röhrig, ed., *Der Gerechte erbarmt sich seines Viehs: Stimmen zur Mitgeschöpflichkeit* (Neukirchen-Vluyn: Neukirchener, 1992). It is also worth mentioning here the Celebration of the Feast of St. Francis that has been happening annually for several years now on October 4 in the Cathedral of St. John the Divine in New York. This celebration, whose culmination is a "blessing of the animals," attracts thousands of human beings, who bring more than a thousand animals. Since not only dogs and cats, but pythons, pigs, eagles, bees, llamas, goldfish, even an elephant or a camel make the pilgrimage to the cathedral, the celebration admittedly becomes a media spectacle. But this by no means makes it an absurdity.

39. Very illuminating in this regard is B. Janowski et al., eds., *Gefährten und Feinde des Menschen: Das Tier in der Lebenswelt des alten Israel* (Neukirchen-Vluyn: Neukirchener, 1993).

40. Cf. the excellent essays by N. Lohfink, "Growth: The Priestly Document and the Limits of Growth," and "The Future: Biblical Witness to

the Ideal of a Stable World," in *Great Themes from the Old Testament*, trans. R. Walls (Edinburgh: T. and T. Clark, 1982), 167–82, 183–201.

## Chapter 6. Creation and Sin

1. D. Bonhoeffer, *Letters and Papers from Prison*, trans. R. H. Fuller, ed. E. Bethge (New York: Macmillan, 1953), 237.

2. Cf. G. Schneider-Flume, *Die Identität des Sünders: Eine Auseinandersetzung theologischer Anthropologie mit dem Konzept der psychosozialen Identität Erik H. Eriksons* (Göttingen: Vandenhoeck, 1985), esp. 25ff., 125ff. On the loss of the doctrine of sin within the framework of the theology of creation, see D. H. Kelsey, "Whatever Happened to the Doctrine of Sin?" *Theology Today* (1993): 169ff.

3. See, e.g., G. W. F. Hegel, *Werke*, ed. E. Moldenhauer and K. M. Michel, vol. 11, *Berliner Schriften Theorie Werkausgabe* (Frankfurt am Main: Suhrkamp, 1970), 239; see also the third *Zusatz* to §24 of the *Encyclopedia* (W. Wallace, trans., *The Logic of Hegel* [Oxford: Clarendon, 1892], 52–57).

4. Hegel, *Berliner Schriften*, 205–74, 239.

5. See also C. Gestrich's subtle presentation of the "aspects of the understanding of sin in modern interpretations of the Yahwistic primeval history in Gen. 2:4bff." (*Die Wiederkehr des Glanzes in der Welt: Die christliche Lehre von der Sünde und ihrer Vergebung in gegenwärtiger Verantwortung* [Tübingen: Mohr, 1989], 102ff; with regard to Hegel, 106ff.).

6. *Werke: Kritische Gesamtausgabe*, vol. 42 (Weimar: Hermann Böhlaus Nachfolger, 1911), 166.

7. J. Calvin, *Commentaries on the First Book of Moses Called Genesis*, vol. 1, trans. J. King (Grand Rapids, Mich.: Eerdmans, n.d.), 182.

8. Ibid., 182, 184. Already in 1523 Philip Melanchthon takes the same position, although less decidedly and with reference back to an earlier tradition of interpretation (C. G. Bretschneider, ed., *Corpus Reformatorum*, vol. 13, 782). Cf. J. Chrysostom in J.-P. Migne, ed., *Patrologia Graecae*, vol. 53, 150ff.

9. Cf. J. Ringleben, *Hegels Theorie der Sünde* (Berlin: De Gruyter, 1977).

10. E. Bloch, *Atheism in Christianity: The Religion of the Exodus and the Kingdom*, trans. J. T. Swann (New York: Herder and Herder, 1972), 86; cf. 85ff., 183ff.

11. H. Gunkel, *Genesis*, 9th ed. (Göttingen: Vandenhoeck, 1977), 29ff. Cf. Gunkel's use of "reason" with that of J. G. Herder, *Sämtliche Werke*, vol. 7, ed. Suphan (1884), 108ff.; see also 28ff., 60 and passim.

12. H. Gese, *Vom Sinai zum Zion: Alttestamentliche Beiträge zur biblischen Theologie* (Munich: Kaiser, 1974), 102–103, 110.

13. O. H. Steck, *Die Paradieserzählung: Eine Auslegung von Genesis 2,b–3,24*, Biblische Studien—Neukirchen (Neukirchen-Vluyn: Neukirchener, 1970), 11, 34ff, 88, 100–101, 103, 107, 116–17, 124–25.

14. C. Westermann, *Genesis 1–11: A Commentary*, trans. J. Scullion (Minneapolis: Augsburg, 1984), 241–42.

15. Ibid., 241.

16. Ibid.

17. Ibid., 242, trans. altered.

18. A. H. J. Gunneweg seems to want to emphasize this ("Schluld ohne Vergebung?" *Evangelische Theologie* 36 [1976]: 8).

19. Steck, *Paradieserzählung*, 34, n. 43.

20. Westermann, *Genesis*, 242, trans. altered.

21. Gese, *Vom Sinai zum Zion*, 102.

22. Steck, *Paradieserzählung*, 35, n. 43; cf. 129.

23. Cf. W. Trillhaas, "Felix culpa: Zur Deutung der Geschichte vom Sündenfall bei Hegel," in H. W. Wolff, ed., *Probleme biblischer Theologie: Gerhard von Rad zum 70. Geburtstag* (Munich: Chr. Kaiser, 1971), 589ff.

24. W. Schmidt, "Anthropologische Begriffe im Alten Testament: Anmerkungen zum hebräischen Denken," *Evangelische Theologie* 24 (1964): 374ff., 387.

25. See chap. 1 above.

26. Cf. M. H. Suchocki, *The Fall to Violence: Original Sin in Relational Theology* (New York: Continuum, 1994), 101ff.

# index